Peace In Every Storm

Declarations & Meditations for Difficult Times

Bill & Beni Johnson

16pt

Copyright Page from the Original Book

BroadStreet Publishing Group, LLC. Savage, Minnesota, USA Broadstreetpublishing.com

PEACE IN EVERY STORM
© 2021 by Bill & Beni Johnson

All rights reserved. No part of this publication may be reproduced, distributed, or transmitted in any form or by any means, including photocopying, recording, or other electronic or mechanical methods, without the prior written permission of the publisher, except in the case of brief quotations embodied in critical reviews and certain other noncommercial uses permitted by copyright law.

Scripture quotations marked (NLT) are taken from the Holy Bible, New Living Translation, copyright © 1996, 2004, 2007. Used by permission of Tyndale House Publishers, Inc., Carol Stream, Illinois 60188. All rights reserved. Scripture quotations marked (NIV) are taken from the Holy Bible, New International Version®, NIV®. Copyright © 1973, 1978, 1984, 2011 by Biblica, Inc.™ Used by permission of Zondervan. All rights reserved worldwide. zondervan.com. The "NIV" and "New International Version" are trademarks registered in the United States Patent and Trademark Office by Biblica, Inc. Scripture quotations marked (NASB) are taken from the New American Standard Bible®, Copyright © 1960, 1971, 1972, 1977, 1995, 2020 by The Lockman Foundation. Used by permission. Lockman.org. Scripture quotations marked (ESV) are from the ESV® Bible (The Holy Bible, English Standard Version®), copyright © 2001 by Crossway, a publishing ministry of Good News Publishers. Used by permission. All rights reserved. Scripture quotations marked (NKJV) are taken from the New King James Version®. Copyright © 1982 by Thomas Nelson. Used by permission. All rights reserved. Scripture quotations marked (AMP) are taken from the Amplified Bible, Copyright © 1954, 1958, 1962, 1964, 1965, 1987 by The Lockman Foundation. Used by permission. Scripture quotations marked (MSG) are taken from The Message. Copyright © by Eugene H. Peterson 1993, 1994, 1995, 1996, 2000, 2001, 2002. Used by permission of Tyndale House Publishers, Inc. Scripture quotations marked (TPT) are taken from The Passion Translation®. Copyright © 2020 by Passion & Fire Ministries, Inc. Used by permission of BroadStreet Publishing. All rights reserved.

Design by Chris Garborg | garborgdesign.com
Editing by Michelle Winger | literallyprecise.com

TABLE OF CONTENTS

THE FINAL SAY	1
REDUCED TO STRENGTH	4
PEACE IS A PERSON	7
LOVE VS FEAR	10
PRAYERS OF AUTHORITY	13
DENYING INFLUENCE	16
FAITH IN CRISIS	19
THE MIND OF CHRIST	22
BIBLICAL MEDITATION	25
STRENGTHEN YOURSELF IN HIM	29
TO DO THE IMPOSSIBLE	32
KEEP DREAMING	35
PREPARED FOR VICTORY	38
THE DECISION POINT	41
INVITATION FOR BREAKTHROUGH	44
BEYOND UNDERSTANDING	47
PAIN AND DISAPPOINTMENT	50
RADICAL GENEROSITY	53
STRENGTH FOUND IN JOY	56
STRONGHOLDS OF THOUGHT	59
OTHER SIDE OF THE STORM	62
A SUPERIOR TRUTH	65
LIVING WITH MYSTERY	68
EYES ON GOD	71
SUPERNATURAL COURAGE	74
SHELTERED IN HIS GOODNESS	77
THE POWER OF TRUST	80
FROM OUR KNEES	83
CONTENDING VS RESTING	86

ABANDONING INTROSPECTION	89
FAMILY FIRST	92
CONFESS AND DECLARE	95
THE FATHER OF FAITH	98
WORSHIP OR WORRY	101
GATES OF PRAISE	104
CONTINUAL DEVOTION	107
FRUITFULNESS IN PRAISE	110
WINDS OF ADVERSITY	113
FAITH-FILLED HEART	116
A UNITED PEOPLE	119
REJOICE ALWAYS	122
IN THE SHELTER OF THE ALMIGHTY	125
SUPERNATURAL HOPE	128
NO OTHER OPTION	131
DIVINE PURPOSE	134
HIDDEN IN HIM	137
SOWING SEED FOR THE FUTURE	140
BEAUTY FOR ASHES	143
THE PEACE OF GOD	146
CALL UPON THE LORD	149
PETER'S PRAYER	152
GOD OF ABUNDANCE	155
BACK COVER MATERIAL	160

When a storm is raging around you, it can be easy to feel overwhelmed. As you read these pages, our prayer is that you would find an anchor of God's goodness, His faithfulness, and His protection no matter what your circumstances. God is with you. He is for you. He is not intimidated by the size of the waves that surround you or the howling winds that threaten to shake you.

Psalms says that His "wrap-around presence is our defense" (84:9 TPT). And Jesus promised that His Spirit would bring us comfort and truth. We have been given His peace—a peace that surpasses our ability to understand—to safeguard our hearts and minds (see Philippians 4:7).

As you read these entries and meditate on the Scriptures, let His voice become the loudest thing in the room. Hide yourself in His strength. You can be confident that you've been given the grace for victory in everything you are facing. God is fighting your battles. You are His beloved child, and He is eternally worthy of your trust.

Bill & Beni Johnson

THE FINAL SAY

"Everything I've taught you is so that the peace which is in me will be in you and will give you great confidence as you rest in me. For in this unbelieving world you will experience trouble and sorrows, but you must be courageous, for I have conquered the world!"
JOHN 16:33 TPT

The last chapter has been written, and we win!

There is no permanent victory for the devil. Ever. Imagine Satan's response, thinking that he'd won a final victory when the Messiah was crucified only to realize the trouble he was in three days later. There are a couple of things that are guaranteed to you. First, every situation where you have ever experienced the devourer—the one who kills, steals, and destroys—will be worked for your benefit (see Romans 8:28). Did God design your suffering? No. It wasn't His idea, but He's so big that He can win with any hand. He will take any situation that comes into our lives with affliction and turn it around for our blessing.

Here's the second thing: our God is the God of vengeance (see Psalm 94:1). There's no such thing as the devil having the final say in anything.

That beast will be silenced and there will be absolute vindication for every moment of infirmity, affliction, torment, pain, and temptation you've ever experienced.

God draws near in judgment (see Malachi 3:5) not to condemn us, but to judge the powers of hell. There will be vindication. Even if you don't see it all in this world, there's just a thin veil that separates this world from eternity. You will have the pleasure of seeing the vindication of God for every single bit of loss you've ever experienced.

Finally, Romans 8:18 (NASB) says, "The sufferings of this present time are not worthy to be compared with the glory that is to be revealed to us." It is not worthy of comparison. Whatever difficulty you have experienced or are currently experiencing, it cannot be compared to the glory that will be revealed in you, on you, and through you. Like Bob Mumford said, "I read the last chapter, and we win."

> When the perishable has been clothed with the imperishable, and the mortal with immortality, then the saying that is written will come true: "Death has been swallowed up in victory."
>
> I CORINTHIANS 15:54 NIV

✷✷✷

Have you seen God redeem situations in your life in the past? List them out,

remembering His faithfulness. If you were to write a final chapter of your life—filled with God's vindication—what would it look like?

REDUCED TO STRENGTH

Then the LORD said to Gideon, "There are too many people with you for Me to hand over Midian to them, otherwise Israel will boast [about themselves] against Me, saying, 'My own power has rescued me.'"
JUDGES 7:2 AMP

God will reduce me to my place of strength.

Gideon had an assignment from the Lord. He was to leave his hiding place and lead Israel's army into battle with the Midianites. God brought an army of men to him, but almost immediately He began to send people back home. The strength of Gideon would not come from the number of his troops. God often prunes us back to a place of strength and health found in our dependence on Him. It's not pleasant, but our comfort is not His main concern.

Israel had 32,000 soldiers. With those numbers, they could have taken credit for the victory God had for them.

God was going to reduce the army to a mere 300 men. First, He sent home the 22,000 men who were fearful. Fear makes people unstable and more likely to take glory for themselves. God is jealous for His glory, and fear turns the attention away from the greatness of God and back onto our own ability.

With 10,000 people left, God had one more test; He was only going to select the men who drank water in a specific way. It would be so nice if every time God gave us a test we knew what the goal was. If the king who only hit the ground with the arrows three times had known God's goal in testing him, he probably would've hit the ground a million times (see 2 Kings 13:18).

But God doesn't do that. He puts us in the middle of a test, and He tests for something that we can't fake—character. When the 10,000 went to the water, 9,700 drank directly from the river and 300 scooped the water into their mouths, staying alert. God chose the latter.

The Lord could've won that battle on His own without any army, so He wasn't demonstrating that He could be victorious with only a few men. He was showing that He would bring victory, no matter how many in number, with those who weren't fearful and who were alert. Now Gideon's army was ready. God had reduced them to their place of strength.

He said to me, "My grace is sufficient for you, for my power is made perfect in weakness." Therefore I will boast all the more gladly about my weaknesses, so that Christ's power may rest

on me. That is why, for Christ's sake, I delight in weaknesses, in insults, in hardships, in persecutions, in difficulties. For when I am weak, then I am strong.
2 CORINTHIANS 12:9-10 NIV

***

Where have you experienced the reduction of God? How has that caused you to depend on His strength even more?

PEACE IS A PERSON

"Peace I leave with you, My peace I give to you; not as the world gives do I give to you. Let not your heart be troubled, neither let it be afraid."
JOHN 14:27 NKJV

God's peace prevails over every situation in my life because the Person of Peace lives within me.

If we look around us at the circumstances—political, economic, social—the enemy has succeeded in raising up voices that best represent hopelessness. It doesn't take much. We can simply turn on the news to immediately hear all that is wrong with the world. It is hard to find a voice of hope and easy to find hopelessness. Some give it a different name, calling it discernment, realism, or intelligence. But, whatever name it's given, hopelessness is not a part of God's kingdom. His intention for this world is to fill it with His presence. The angels declared, "Glory to God in the highest, and on earth peace, goodwill toward men!" (Luke 2:14) That is the will of God.

Peace is the prevailing substance of the atmosphere of heaven, and God has given us His *shalom*—everything coming into alignment with Him—as our inheritance. Peace is not the absence of something. It's not the absence of war, fear, or noise. True peace is the presence of Someone. It's the Prince of Peace who crushes the powers of darkness under our feet when we become permeated with Him. It is Peace Himself who offers Himself as the Comforter so we might never need to be afraid. It is for peace that God gave us His Son so we might taste of eternity. How could we know that and choose to live without hope?

Though we can look at the circumstances of the world and feel overwhelmed, we are not here to announce the enemy's victory; we are here to announce his defeat. The same Spirit that raised Christ from the dead dwells in us. Hopelessness has been defeated. His peace—that which touches us spirit, soul, and body—tames every opposition. God's peace prevails over every situation in our lives because the Person of Peace lives within us.

Now, may the Lord himself, the Lord of peace, pour into you his peace in every circumstance and in every possible way. The Lord's tangible presence be with you all.
1 THESSALONIANS 3:16 TPT

***

Where do you see the world's greatest need for the Person of Peace to invade? List some of the breakthrough that would

result from heaven invading these situations.

LOVE VS FEAR

"Do not fear, for I am with you; Do not be afraid, for I am your God. I will strengthen you, I will also help you, I will also uphold you with My righteous right hand."
ISAIAH 41:10 NASB

What I fear will influence what I worship, and what I worship will be proven by what I trust.

"Do not fear" is the commandment repeated more often than any other in Scripture. By repeating the commandment so frequently, the Lord reveals the primary tactic the enemy uses to disengage us from our life source. The devil can't cut us off from God; he's not that powerful. But he can tempt us out of alignment with our Creator. Like a dislocated arm that no longer has full mobility, we can become disjointed, not functioning in our intended authority. And fear is what does that.

Fear is an agreement with the enemy. Any time we believe a lie, we empower the liar. We don't want to become devil-focused, but as Paul writes to the Corinthians, we can't be "ignorant of his schemes" (2 Corinthians 2:11). When the Lord says, "Do not fear," He is never trying to shame or expose us. Rather, He's revealing to us that the grace to be victorious over fear is within our reach. He is inviting us into a partnership. When He gives commands, He enables us to do what we previously couldn't do. That is the empowering nature of grace.

There is grace to deal with whatever comes against us. Experiencing fear is not a sin, but partnering with it—embracing fear as though it were truth—is a violation of God's design. This doesn't mean we ignore the reality of our circumstances. It means that, in the midst of our circumstances, we recognize there is a higher reality. Jesus has taken care of every problem we could ever face. We now walk in His victory, aligning our minds with His. What we fear will influence what we worship, and what we worship will be proven by what we trust.

> Don't worry about anything; instead, pray about everything. Tell God what you need, and thank him for all he has done. Then you will experience God's peace, which exceeds anything we can understand. His peace will guard your hearts and minds as you live in Christ Jesus.
> PHILIPPIANS 4:6-7 NLT

***

How has fear tried to disconnect you from God's goodness, power, and vision for your life? Take some time to remind yourself

that God is bigger than any fearful smokescreen the enemy could throw up before your destiny. You have a powerful destiny and calling on your life.

PRAYERS OF AUTHORITY

The God of peace will soon crush Satan under your feet.
ROMANS 16:20 NIV

I can only release peace over a storm through which I can sleep.

Jesus and the disciples got into a boat to cross the Sea of Galilee. As they were crossing, they ran into a storm so strong that the disciples knew they'd most likely die. They were terrified. They woke up Jesus, the Son of God, and pleaded with Him to do something to save them. They cried out just like many of us pray when we're in the middle of a crisis: "Don't you care if we drown?" (Mark 4:38) But Jesus rebuked them for their lack of faith.

What they didn't realize was that if Jesus was sleeping in their boat, they had divine purpose no matter the strength of the storm. Jesus was asleep because He lives from the kingdom of heaven toward earth. And in His kingdom, there is no turmoil. When the disciples cried out to Him, He woke up and commanded the wind and waves to stop. He rebuked the wind and declared peace over the waves. The chaos stopped immediately.

Many people could have stood at the bow of the boat, rebuking the storm to no avail because they were ministering out of fear. But Jesus was able to release peace because He lived *in* peace. Peace is a military move that overwhelms and subdues the demonic. The *shalom* of heaven subdues all chaos.

Jesus slept during the storm because He was a citizen of heaven in the same way that we are. Sometimes we imagine that, in prayer, we are trying to get God to intervene. In fact, God is looking for people to use the authority they've been given. Instead of reaching out to God, trying to get Him to invade our circumstances, we are to boldly pray from the promises of God. When we can see our circumstance from heaven's perspective, we have the authority and anointing to address the problem. We can only release peace over a storm through which we can sleep. He told them, "It was because of your lack of faith. I promise you, if you have faith inside of you no bigger than the size of a small mustard seed, you can say to this mountain, 'Move away from here and go over there,' and you will see it move! There is nothing you couldn't do!"

MATTHEW 17:20 TPT

***

15

What storms in your life are trying to distract you from the divine purpose of God on your life? How can you reconnect with the peace of heaven in order to pray with authority?

DENYING INFLUENCE

"I am Yahweh, your mighty God! I grip your right hand and won't let you go! I whisper to you: 'Don't be afraid; I am here to help you!'"
ISAIAH 41:13 TPT

Faith doesn't deny a problem exists; it denies it a place of influence.

Sometimes, those of us who work hard to develop a culture of faith can unintentionally begin to live in denial. We can pretend that certain problems or challenges don't exist. But that's not a healthy way to live. It doesn't develop our capacity to address the things that are going on in and around us.

If we examine a problem deeply and honestly, we can gain understanding about it and what needs to change. But we don't stop there. We then listen to what God is saying. We look over the words God has spoken to us in the recent months to find the tools or insight He has given us in order to help us address the current problem.

God doesn't put us in situations where we are ill-equipped. We may feel like we are, but if we stop being intimidated by the size of a problem and begin to examine our history with God, we will generally see that God has been empowering us for whatever situation in which we find ourselves.

Fear causes us to forget the tools that God has put in our possession. When we can step out of fear and remember who God is, we refuse to allow the problem to influence our thinking, emotions, and value systems. If we can succeed there, we will begin to discover the tools God has already put in our lives—the revelations, the promises, and the instructions that will take us into the seasons of breakthrough we long for.

We never have to be afraid because He has seen the end from the beginning (see Isaiah 46:10). He has every solution. Whatever problem we are facing doesn't catch God off guard. He knows ahead of time the very things that are coming our way, and He prepares us to face them victoriously. He created us to be an overcoming community of believers; it's our nature in God. Trusting Him is what defines us. Faith doesn't deny a problem exists; it denies it a place of influence.

Trust in and rely confidently on the LORD with all your heart And do not rely on your own insight or understanding. In all your ways know and acknowledge and recognize Him, And He will make your paths straight and smooth [removing obstacles that block your way].
PROVERBS 3:5-6 AMP

***

What problem are you facing that you need God's wisdom to navigate? Think back through your last year with Him. What things has He been teaching and equipping you with that you can use to address this current issue?

FAITH IN CRISIS

The fundamental fact of existence is that this trust in God, this faith, is the firm foundation under everything that makes life worth living. It's our handle on what we can't see. The act of faith is what distinguished our ancestors, set them above the crowd. By faith, we see the world called into existence by God's word, what we see created by what we don't see.
HEBREWS 11:1-3 MSG

My faith will take me through the crisis.

The eleventh chapter of Hebrews is sometimes referred to as the faith hall of fame. Many of the great men and women of Scripture, individuals who had accomplished much for God through their faith, are named in this chapter. Abraham, Moses, and Sarah are listed. The mouths of lions and other incredible exploits are mentioned. It's not a complete list, but it highlights the fact that faith is a central theme in Scripture and foundational to our relationship with the Lord. It reveals a God who is moved by our faith.

This chapter in the Bible is a declaration that will last through the ages to honor all of those who have lived by faith. But, after listing names and various exploits for God, the writer of Hebrews shifts the tone to talk about all the problems that faith helped people to walk through. At the end of the chapter, it says, "There were others who were tortured, refusing to be released so that they might gain an even better resurrection" (Hebrews 11:35 NIV).

The faith that enables you to lay hands on someone and see cancer dissolve is the same faith that helps you to stay strong in a crisis. This is huge because often when we're in the midst of a crisis, we tend to examine our faith and find it lacking. More often than not, we think, *I must not have as much faith as so-and-so had.*

In the midst of some of the most astounding examples of faith in the entire Bible, the author shows us people who didn't have immediate answers to their problems. These were people who had to live, like us, between the promise that God had given and the problem that God had not yet answered. Living in the tension between the promise and the miracle, they were kept in a place of humility and dependence on God. And their faith will be celebrated for all of eternity in God's Word. Their faith took them through the crisis.

> I have fought an excellent fight. I have finished my full course with all my might and I've kept my heart full of faith.
>
> 2 TIMOTHY 4:7 TPT

***

Sometimes when we are in the middle of the storm, it's challenging to see our faith-filled decisions the way God does. Spend some time with Him and ask Him what this season of your life looks like through His eyes. What is He counting as faith that you may not consider great faith?

22

THE MIND OF CHRIST

"Heaven's kingdom can be compared to yeast that a woman takes and blends into three measures of flour and then waits until all the dough rises."
MATTHEW 13:33 TPT

My transformed mind will transform my life; my transformed life will transform my city.

The Lord's intention is to daily transform our perception so we live from the mind of Christ. Scripture says that "we have the mind of Christ" (1 Corinthians 2:16 NASB). This is absolutely true. Everything has been purchased for us, but we have many things in our account as believers that are not yet in our possession. It's possible to starve to death with a million dollars in the bank. We have to make withdrawals on what He has placed in our account.

Learning how to make withdrawals—how to recognize truth, act upon it, and grab hold of those things that God has made available to us—is how this adventure with Him becomes fruitful. It is how we change the world for His glory. God is not merely interested in training us to be nice people in an angry world; we are nice people who carry the leaven of the kingdom. Once the leaven gets worked into the dough of the world, it can never be removed.

You can't unleaven dough. All it needs is heat to become leavened bread. Likewise, the heat of our circumstances reveals the kind of leaven we have put into the dough of our lives. We have either folded in the leaven of the kingdom or the leaven of our own opinions. We cannot have both.

The Lord longs for our thought life to reflect His. He said, "Do not be conformed to this world, but be transformed by the renewing of your mind, so that you may prove what the will of God is, that which is good and acceptable and perfect" (Romans 12:2). The transformation of every person is equal to the transformation of our thought life—no more, no less.

We often try to use Christian principles to transform our life, workplace, family, politics, etc. These are worthy goals, but if our minds are not renewed, we lack the authority to change the world around us. It all starts by aligning our thought life with His. A transformed mind transforms a life; a transformed life transforms a city.

> You were taught, with regard to your former way of life, to put off your old self, which is being corrupted by its deceitful desires; to be made new in the attitude of your minds; and to

put on the new self, created to be like God in true righteousness and holiness.
EPHESIANS 4:22-24 NIV

***

When you have experienced the heat of difficult circumstances, what have you learned about yourself? How have you seen the leaven of the kingdom evident in your life, and in what ways has the leaven of the world been revealed? What thought processes do you need to surrender to God?

BIBLICAL MEDITATION

"No one will be able to oppose you all the days of your life. Just as I have been with Moses, I will be with you; I will not desert you nor abandon you. Be strong and courageous, for you shall give this people possession of the land which I swore to their fathers to give them. Only be strong and very courageous; be careful to do according to all the Law which Moses My servant commanded you; do not turn from it to the right or to the left, so that you may achieve success wherever you go. This Book of the Law shall not depart from your mouth, but you shall meditate on it day and night, so that you may be careful to do according to all that is written in it; for then you will make your way prosperous, and then you will achieve success. Have I not commanded you? Be strong and courageous! Do not be terrified nor dismayed, for the LORD your God is with you wherever you go."
JOSHUA 1: 5-9 NASB

Biblical meditation is a source of mental health forever.

This passage of Scripture from Joshua gives us the direction as clearly as possible: be strong and very courageous. We are commanded to be courageous, told that God will make our way prosperous and successful, but the verse doesn't explain how to obtain that courage. At the very end, though, it gives one profound sliver of instruction that makes everything else in the prior verses possible: meditate on this Word day and night. Biblical meditation is one of the most neglected areas of Christian discipline.

Probably all of us have had the experience of being so anxious about something that it runs around in our heads all night, making it impossible to sleep. It's clear that we know how to meditate. We just have to change the subject matter of our meditation.

There is western meditation, which is an intellectual exercise, and there is eastern meditation, where the goal is to empty the mind. Biblical meditation is different. In Hebrew, *meditation* meant to quietly repeat something in a soft, droning sound while utterly abandoning outside distraction. There is a Jewish prayer called *davening* which is the recitation of Scriptures, praying intense prayers, or getting lost in communion with God while bowing or rocking back and forth. If you've ever seen people praying at the Wailing Wall in Israel, you'll know what it looks like.

We are inundated daily with words and constantly bombarded with the values of the world. Meditation is an ongoing encounter with God. It is the experience of harnessing our thoughts and emotions and aligning them with what God is saying. As we do this, we begin to carry the very shape of what God has said.

Joshua's success as a leader depended on him not letting the Word of God depart from his mouth. It was all connected to this one simple assignment: meditation. Our heart, mind, and emotions can be trained in the mind of Christ through biblical meditation. It's a source of mental health forever.

What delight comes to the one who follows
God's ways! He won't walk in step with the wicked, nor share the sinner's way, nor be found
sitting in the scorner's seat. His passion is to remain true to the Word of "I Am," meditating day and night on the true revelation of light. He will be standing firm like a flourishing tree planted
by God's design, deeply rooted by the brooks of bliss, bearing fruit in every season of life.
PSALM 1:1-3 TPT

***

What are some of your favorite Bible verses that encourage and strengthen you? Do you have any of them memorized? How can you place these verses in front of you

throughout your day so you can meditate on God's Word?

STRENGTHEN YOURSELF IN HIM

Those who wait on the LORD Shall renew their strength; They shall mount up with wings like eagles, They shall run and not be weary, They shall walk and not faint.
ISAIAH 40:31 NKJV

In the face of challenges, I will find God's goodness and give Him praise.

It's not possible for us to come into God's intended destiny without learning how to navigate disappointment, loss, and pain. David is a great example of this. Before he became king, he experienced a string of intense rejection and disappointment. It would be reasonable to think that if a prophet came along and anointed you with oil, ordaining you as the king, your life might change fairly soon. But it took somewhere between ten and thirteen years before David became king.

In that time, he was forced to run for his life from Saul. He left Israel to live with Philistines. He tried to fight against Israel but was rejected by the Philistines. And, to top it off, he returned home with his men to find it utterly destroyed. David's men—the broken men he had turned into warriors—saw the loss of their homes and families. They experienced such pain and grief that they plotted to kill David. He had been rejected by Saul, by Israel, by the Philistines, and now he was being rejected by the very guys he'd poured his life into. This is the moment where everything in David was tested.

Scripture says, "David strengthened himself in the LORD his God" (1 Samuel 30:6). In the very next scene, he became king. Our destiny is often found on the other side of learning how to minister to ourselves in the midst of pain. This isn't an invitation to independence or withdrawal from spiritual community. It's about God teaching us how to embrace our destiny and strengthen ourselves in Him.

We strengthen ourselves by reading through the Psalms until we can hear our heart's cry and experience the Lord's love for us. We turn from away from every thought that erodes our faith in God. Instead, we embrace His Word, sing out the truth, and declare His promises over our circumstances. Our place of great personal strength will be found when, in the face of challenges, we find God's goodness and give Him praise.

We are reborn into a perfect inheritance that can never perish, never be defiled, and never diminish. It is promised and preserved forever in the heavenly realm for you! Through our faith, the mighty power of God constantly guards us until our full salvation is ready to be revealed in the last time. May the thought of this cause you to jump for joy, even though lately you've had to put up with the grief of many trials. I PETER 1:4-6 TPT

***

When you have faced rejection and disappointment, from where were you able to draw strength? Take some time to intentionally praise God for His goodness and faithfulness. What are a few practical tools that would help you strengthen yourself in the Lord the next time you are in pain?

TO DO THE IMPOSSIBLE

He answered and said, "It is written, 'Man shall not live by bread alone, but by every word that proceeds from the mouth of God.'"
MATTHEW 4:4 NKJV

God's Word enables me to do the impossible.

One of the most fundamental parts of the gospel is that God commands things from us that are actually impossible for us to do. He says, "Heal the sick, cleanse the lepers, raise the dead, cast out demons" (Matthew 10:8). We can't do any of these things. But when He commands us to do the impossible, He enables us to do what He has required us to do. The law requires; God's grace enables.

The angel of the Lord appeared to Mary to tell her she was going to bear the Christ child. When she asked how that would be possible, the angel replied, "With God nothing will be impossible" (Luke 1:37). That phrase illustrates a part of the gospel that is so critical for us. We are to anchor our hearts in the Word of God, both what He is saying in the Scripture and what He highlights to us with His voice. His voice will always be confirmed by His written Word.

Jack Taylor explained the verse in Luke in a fascinating way. The word *nothing* is made up of the word *no* but also the word *thing*, which in this case is *rhema*. That word, *rhema*, is often used to talked about the freshly spoken Word of God in Scripture. This then means that "no freshly spoken Word of God will be impossible." The word *impossible* is translated "without ability." So, this verse can actually be translated like this: "No freshly spoken Word of God will ever come to you that does not contain its own ability to perform itself." That's amazing.

James says, "In humility receive the word implanted, which is able to save your souls" (James 1:21 NASB). This is not only referring to the moment of conversion—we are saved, yes, but we are also being saved (see 2 Corinthians 3:18) and someday we will be fully saved (see 1 Corinthians 15:51). The implanted Word of God is able to save, transform, and enable us to do what we normally could not do on our own. His Word enables us to do the impossible.

He died for us, sacrificing himself to make us holy and pure, cleansing us through the showering of the pure water of the Word of God.
EPHESIANS 5:25-26 TPT

***

What has God been highlighting to you in the Scripture? What has He been speaking

into your life recently? How could you choose to actively trust that He is able to bring about that which He promises? What is He enabling you to do?

KEEP DREAMING

"Ask, and the gift is yours. Seek, and you'll discover. Knock, and the door will be opened for you. For every persistent one will get what he asks for. Every persistent seeker will discover what he longs for. And everyone who knocks persistently will one day find an open door."
MATTHEW 7:7-8 TPT

God wants to show the world who He is through my fulfilled dreams.

Some friends of ours went to Lebanon many years ago with the dream to lead and direct a TV ministry, broadcasting the gospel to that part of the world. When they arrived, though, that region fell into conflict. Everything seemed to collapse around them, but they didn't retreat. Instead, they pivoted.

With the television program no longer an option, they shifted to developing a correspondence course that sent the message of the gospel into dark places of the earth. Because of that course, the gospel spread like wildfire. God had given them the desire to work in television in Lebanon, but the real desire was to spread the gospel throughout the middle east. And He knew how to best make that happen.

Their dream had been born of God, even though the initial expression seemed to be a failure. Their idea for the television show had positioned them perfectly to discover how God was actually going to unfold the deep desire of their hearts, sharing the gospel in hard-to-reach areas. Staying flexible but persistent with their dreams allowed Him to answer the cry of their hearts in the way He knew would be best.

Every dream in your heart is significant. Every dream at its core was born of God. The particular expression of your dream may not be of Him, but God invites us to dream freely with Him. Keep an ongoing list of dreams, without distinguishing between the spiritual and the non-spiritual, and offer them to Him, watching how He moves.

Our dreams become real estate that God occupies. He made each of us as a unique expression, so it would be a sad waste to pressure ourselves to dream only what we think we should. Trust that your imagination has been redeemed; Dream what you dream—everything from a special vacation with your family to seeing the dead raised—and watch as He uses natural things to bring about a supernatural impact. God wants to show the world who He is through the fulfilled dreams of His kids.

The eye of the LORD is upon those who fear

Him [and worship Him with awe-inspired reverence and obedience], On those who hope

[confidently] in His compassion and lovingkindness.
PSALM 33:18 AMP

***

What dreams are in your heart to accomplish? Ask yourself what the heart is behind those dreams? Why do you want to do the thing you long to do? What aspect of God's heart will be revealed to the world when your dream is fulfilled?

PREPARED FOR VICTORY

"The LORD will fight for you while you [only need to] keep silent and remain calm."
EXODUS 14:14 AMP

There is no circumstance I face for which He has not prepared me.

The Israelites were freed from slavery in Egypt and God led them through the desert toward the Promised Land. It took them forty years, not because of the geography but because the Lord was retraining them. They had carried the identity of slaves for generations, but God wanted to instill the ways of His kingdom so they could not only enter but also inhabit their land of promise. As the saying goes, "It was easy to get Israel out of Egypt, but it was hard to get Egypt out of Israel."

Sometimes that meant avoiding conflict: "So it happened, when Pharaoh let the people go, God did not lead them by way of the land of the Philistines, even though it was nearer; for God said, 'The people might change their minds when they see war [that is, that there will be war], and return to Egypt'" (Exodus 13:17). God was the One fighting their battles; it wasn't as if their victory against the Philistines depended on their own wisdom and strength. But God knew that His role would be limited by their fear.

He didn't take them the direct route through the desert because the Israelites weren't prepared—mentally, emotionally, or spiritually. He chose to protect the inexperienced Israelites from the enemy. It wasn't a question if He could win; there's never been a contest between the devil and God. He took them around the battle so their fear wouldn't send them back into bondage.

What does that teach us about the Lord? It shows us that He creates detours around battles we are not fully equipped to win. So, if He hasn't delivered us out of a situation, we can know that He has complete confidence that He has prepared us for victory. When we choose fear instead of faith in the midst of conflict, we violate our design by not acknowledging the divine orchestration of a moment that might, once again, illustrate the victory of Christ. There is no circumstance we face for which He has not prepared us.

"The LORD your God, who goes before you, will Himself fight for you, just as He did for you in Egypt before your eyes, and in the wilderness where you saw how the LORD your God carried you, just as a man carries his son, on all of the

road which you have walked until you came to this place."
DEUTERONOMY 1:30-31 NASB

***

If it is not immediately clear to you how God has prepared you for your current battle, spend some time now and ask Him to show you the ways He has equipped you for this moment. What things have you learned about God that makes trusting Him through this season easier?

THE DECISION POINT

Arise, shine; For your light has come! And the glory of the LORD is risen upon you. For behold, the darkness shall cover the earth, And deep darkness the people; But the LORD will arise over you, And His glory will be seen upon you. The Gentiles shall come to your light, And kings to the brightness of your rising.
ISAIAH 60:1-3 NKJV

I will be equipped for battle by facing conflict with integrity and faith.

There is always a decision point: What are we going to do in the face of conflict? The decisions we make in those moments determine whether we will benefit from the trial or be undermined by it. God will fully prepare us for what He is doing on the earth. He has determined that everything would be used to promote the gospel, increase His lordship in our lives, and develop our effectiveness in this world.

Every bit of opposition is given to us so we might stand and oppose it, revealing to the world that Jesus is greater than the powers of hell. And not only is Jesus greater, but "He who is in you is greater than he who is in the world" (1 John 4:4). In the midst of conflict, God longs to display His sovereignty and His authority through each one of us. Sometimes conflict is confusing because we lose sight of the bigger picture. But when we understand the purpose of trials, it's easier to embrace what God is doing.

God has a wonderful plan for His church; we know the end of the story—we will be triumphant, a glorious Bride, not one surviving by the skin of her teeth (see Ephesians 5:27). Nations are going to cry out for discipleship, hospitals are going to be emptied as people are healed, and we have a strange awareness that we are not fully equipped for the day that is coming.

That day, as bright as it will be, will also be a dark day (see Isaiah 60), and we know we don't have every tool we need. James 1:2-4 tells us the remedy: "My brethren, count it all joy when you fall into various trials, knowing that the testing of your faith produces patience. But let patience have its perfect work, that you may be perfect and complete, lacking nothing." He is equipping us for the battle for which we were born. We get that way by facing conflict with integrity and faith.

May the God who brought us peace by raising from the dead our Lord Jesus Christ so that he would be the Great Shepherd of his flock; and
by the power of the blood of the eternal covenant may he work perfection into every part

of you giving you all that you need to fulfill your destiny. And may he express through you all that is excellent and pleasing to him through your life-union with Jesus the Anointed One who is to receive all glory forever! Amen!
HEBREWS 13:20-21 TPT

***

Spend time with God and ask Him how He wants to reveal His sovereignty and authority through you in the midst of this trial. What tools is He placing in your hands? How could you increase your integrity and faith during this time?

INVITATION FOR BREAKTHROUGH

"I will give you the keys of the kingdom of heaven; and whatever you bind on earth shall have been bound in heaven, and whatever you loose on earth shall have been loosed in heaven."
MATTHEW 16:19 NASB

Every challenge is an invitation for breakthrough.

When the Lord allows a challenge to come our way, it is to reveal our need as an invitation into further breakthrough. If fear, insecurity, or panic rises up in us in the face of a challenge, we can bring that to the feet of Jesus without shame.

Insecurity is just wrong security, exposed. The Lord simply brings to the surface places where we have wrongly positioned our security so we can deal with it and move into a divine solution. There is not one problem on the planet for which Jesus does not have a readily available, well-prepared solution.

Jesus said, "Repent, for the kingdom of heaven is at hand" (Matthew 4:17). The kingdom of heaven is the absolute fulfillment of every single cry of the human heart. Our troubled hearts can be temporarily satisfied in this life by a change in our circumstance. But every longing that we have is only fully satisfied in the realm of the kingdom of God.

So, when Jesus said, "Repent," He was challenging a generation of people to change their perspective so He could free them from living under the influence of an inferior reality. He brought His world with Him, and He invites us to enter in. His kingdom is the dominion of the Almighty God where all is brought into order, where abundant life is manifested, where the peace of God reigns, and where the salvation of the Lord—spirit, soul, and body—is available to us as we turn from the inferior and embrace His way.

In Acts, Peter and John came to a gate and saw a lame man begging for alms. Peter said, "I do not have silver and gold, but what I do have I give to you: In the name of Jesus Christ the Nazarene, walk!" (Acts 3:6) Peter didn't have money, but he had the name of Jesus: the name to which every power of destruction, sickness, and death must bow. The kingdom of heaven touched him, and the man left walking, leaping, and praising God. Every challenge is an invitation for breakthrough.

The kingdom of God is not a matter of eating and drinking, but of righteousness, peace and joy in the Holy Spirit.

ROMANS 14:17 NIV

***

What has risen up in your heart when you are in the middle of a challenge? From your reaction, where do you see you need God to bring breakthrough? If you experienced fear or insecurity, how would your life be different if you were free of those feelings?

BEYOND UNDERSTANDING

Don't be pulled in different directions or worried about a thing. Be saturated in prayer throughout each day, offering your faith-filled requests before God with overflowing gratitude. Tell him every detail of your life, then God's wonderful peace that transcends human understanding, will guard your heart and mind through Jesus Christ.
PHILIPPIANS 4:6-7 TPT

My heart will take me where my head can't fit.

Many people—whether or not they have a relationship with God—can be kind, generous, and loving. But there is something that only a believer can offer: the reality of another world that reshapes the reality of this one. Jesus said that His words were spirit and life (see John 6:63). In other words, He was telling the disciples that His words become presence and that His presence gives life. It's life-giving even when we don't understand what He's doing.

In John 6, Jesus preached a message that clearly would not have been chosen for heaven's PR campaign. He told a large crowd that they would have to eat His flesh and drink His blood in order to participate in eternal life (see verse 53). He was saying what the Father was saying and doing what He was doing. But here God was saying something that no one could understand.

If there were ever a culture that would be anti-cannibalism, it would be Israel. You can imagine the crowd's response: "Was this the same guy who was multiplying food earlier?" The crowd soon began to leave. This is church growth at its finest: a crowd of 15,000 people dwindled down to the twelve disciples.

Jesus then turned to the twelve and asked them if they were going to leave too. But Peter understood: "Lord, where would we go? No one but you gives us the revelation of eternal life" (John 6:68). In other words, he said, "Jesus, we don't understand the flesh and blood thing any more than the crowd that left. But what we do know is that every time You speak, we come alive inside." If we can only accept the things of God that we understand, we've created a god in our own image.

We never want to reduce God to our size, to our limitations and restrictions. Every follower of Jesus needs to have moments when they choose to follow Him purely out of trust instead of understanding. Christianity is not called "the understanding;" it is called "the faith." Our hearts will take us where our heads can't fit.

"My thoughts are not your thoughts, neither are your ways my ways," declares the LORD. "For as the heavens are higher than the earth, so are my ways higher than your ways and my thoughts than your thoughts."
ISAIAH 55:8-9 ESV

***

What are some things of God that you do not understand? Are those mysteries pulling you away from God, or are they driving you deeper into His presence? Quiet your mind and allow Him to speak to you today. Offer up your complete trust to Him once again.

PAIN AND DISAPPOINTMENT

LORD, sustain me as you promised, that I may live! Do not let my hope be crushed.
PSALM 119:116 NLT

I am shaped by my decision to honor God in every situation.

Every single person has dealt with pain and disappointment in their lives. There are no real solutions to loss and devastation apart from the presence of God. But there are a few things that we can do to sustain our hearts, reconnecting with peace in the middle of chaos and loss.

First, we need to get alone with God. Without accusing Him, we can express how we're feeling with absolute honesty. We don't need to make ourselves presentable for God as if He doesn't already know what's going on in our hearts. If it feels like He's betrayed you, left you alone, or abandoned you, tell Him. He invites us into His presence as we are; we get to pour out our hearts to Him about the pain we're feeling.

Then, we must remind ourselves about who we know Him to be. We may be feeling alone, betrayed, or deceived, but we know that He is not a Father who abandons, betrays, or lies. He is faithful; He is always good. He doesn't owe us any explanation. We will serve Him with joy regardless of our situations, but we can show Him our pain and confess what we know to be true about Him.

We can then turn to His Word. Sometimes, He may give us an impression of where to read. Other times, we can go to a familiar passage where He's previously spoken to our hearts. Or we can simply begin to read until He speaks to us. When He speaks, we may not have an answer for the situation we're in, but we will have an answer for the pain in our hearts.

Seasons of grief allow us to hold up our biggest disappointments to the Lord and intentionally offer Him a sacrifice of praise for who He is. Our pain and loss get to flavor our worship. This is an offering we won't have a chance to give Him in heaven. We only have this life to give Him that gift. And we are shaped by our decision to honor Him in every situation.

Though He slay me, I will hope in Him. Nevertheless I will argue my ways before Him.
JOB 13:15 NASB

***

Is it easy or challenging for you to share your heart openly and honestly with God?

Take some time to authentically share with Him how you are feeling. Once you've done that, declare who you know Him to be. Find evidence of His goodness in His Word.

RADICAL GENEROSITY

"Give generously and generous gifts will be given back to you, shaken down to make room for more. Abundant gifts will pour out upon you with such an overflowing measure that it will run over the top! The measurement of your generosity becomes the measurement of your return."
LUKE 6:38 TPT

I face each challenge in the opposite spirit, pouring out generosity in the face of lack.

In Acts, prophets came to Antioch to warn the early church of an impending worldwide famine (see 11:28). As soon as the disciples heard this news, they responded with generosity: "They determined that each believer, according to his or her ability, would give an offering to send as relief to the brothers living in Judea" (11:29). Remember, the famine was going to affect the whole world, so that meant the disciples knew that scarcity was about to impact their lives. And the first thing they did was tithe. That is remarkable.

Most people, hearing that a famine was about to hit, would retreat, gather to themselves, and do whatever they could to survive. Instead, the disciples moved quickly to take an offering to send to the brethren of Judea. They each gave according to their abilities; there was no manipulation or coercion. There was just an overwhelming thankfulness for God's promises. Their absolute trust in Him prompted them to plant a seed of radical generosity.

The people in this congregation had most likely heard the good news and been converted because ministers of the gospel had traveled from Judea. When they took the offering for them, it was probably a gift of compassion at the news of the famine, but it was also a gift honoring their spiritual heritage.

While the famine did happen, we never hear about it again. There is something so powerful about radical acts of generosity in times of personal need. We can refuse to bow to the threats of the enemy, refuse to succumb to a spirit of fear, and instead aggressively sow into the lives of others, displaying honor rather than succumbing to self-preservation.

After defeating the Philistines, God identifies Himself in David's life as the *Baal-perazim:* God of the breakthrough (see 1 Chronicles 14:11). When there is an obstacle, He breaks through. When there is a season of lack or difficulty, He brings His abundance. He's the God of answers regardless of the problem. Because of Him, we are able to face each challenge in the opposite spirit, pouring out generosity in the face of lack.

Calling his disciples to him, Jesus said, "Truly I tell you, this poor widow has put more into the treasury than all the others. They all gave out of their wealth; but she, out of her poverty, put in everything—all she had to live on."
MARK 12:43-44 NIV

***

What motivates your acts of generosity? Have you ever given a gift in order to honor your spiritual heritage like the early church gave to Judea? Consider the challenge you are facing. What would acting in the opposite spirit look like? What is radical generosity for you today?

STRENGTH FOUND IN JOY

You will show me the path of life; In Your presence is fullness of joy; In Your right hand there are pleasures forevermore.
PSALM 16:11 AMP

My level of strength will be measured according to my level of joy.

In the book of Nehemiah, Israel had finally rebuilt their temples and, with Nehemiah's help, they began to rebuild the city wall. The name Nehemiah actually means *comforter*. He's an unusual depiction of the Holy Spirit in this story. Without him, Israel hadn't been able to rebuild the wall for decades. With Nehemiah, they completed the project in a matter of weeks.

When it was completed, Ezra brought the law of Moses into the public square and the priests read the Scriptures out loud. Men, women, and children stood from sunup to sundown, listening to God's Word in Hebrew. For the first time in their lives, they heard God's requirements. And, as they realized how far they'd been living from God's standard, they began to weep and mourn.

Their response seems appropriate, but Nehemiah corrected them: "This day is holy to the LORD your God. Do not mourn or weep. Go and enjoy choice food and sweet drinks, and send some to those who have nothing prepared. This day is holy to our LORD. Do not grieve, for the joy of the LORD is your strength" (Nehemiah 8:9-10 NIV).

Even though they'd missed the mark, he told them not to mourn. The day was holy and, because of that, they were to have a feast. Joy was important enough that they scheduled it; they planned a celebration *before* they had measured up to God's requirements. This is the discipline of joy. No matter what our current circumstances, it is within our ability to choose joy.

Sorrow, grief, and confession of sins are all important parts of our life in Christ. But here's the problem: we fail to realize the power of this verse: "The joy of the LORD is your strength." Joy was such a huge heavenly commodity that it motivated Jesus to endure the cross (see Hebrews 12:2). Joy is the key to strength; it's a way to health (see Proverbs 17:22); it is evidence of connecting with the presence of God (see Psalm 16:11). Our level of strength will be measured according to our level of joy.

> May the God of hope fill you with all joy and peace as you trust in him, so that you may

overflow with hope by the power of the Holy Spirit.
ROMANS 15:13 NIV

***

If you are feeling in need of strength, try to focus on developing your joy. Even if you don't feel like rejoicing, what could you do that would express joy to God? How could you rejoice with your mind, with your body, and with your spirit? Allow the joy of the Lord to infuse your life with strength!

STRONGHOLDS OF THOUGHT

Though we walk in the flesh, we do not war according to the flesh. For the weapons of our warfare are not carnal but mighty in God for pulling down strongholds, casting down arguments and every high thing that exalts itself against the knowledge of God, bringing every thought into captivity to the obedience of Christ.
2 CORINTHIANS 10:3-5 NKJV

Winning battles internally positions me to influence the world externally.

When our thought life is not aligned with Christ, it not only empowers the enemy, but it also gives him a safe place to hide. When our souls are anchored in trusting something other than God, our thoughts reflect this reality. The weapons of our warfare that Paul speaks of are not our skills or talents; they are the arsenal of God Himself, used to deal with the hiding places of the enemy in our thought life.

The devil knows that, for most of us, he can't get us to deny God's existence. We have too much history with God to fall for that one. But he will try to get us to think about a problem without the hope of a redemptive solution. When that happens, we are exalting something in our thought life that wars against the knowledge of God. There's not a problem we face for which He doesn't already have the answer, and to which He isn't already prepared to release the solution.

Sometimes the more knowledge we have about spiritual realities, the easier it is for us to give fear a spiritual name. When you give a dysfunction a virtuous name, though—calling fear *discernment*, for example—you not only give it permission to remain, but you also give it permission to set down roots until it begins to shape your personality.

The answer isn't to ignore spiritual knowledge, but everything we learn must take us to the person of Jesus Christ. He is the Lamb who will sit on the throne for eternity, giving us a constant reminder of our dependency (see Revelation 5:13).

Pulling down strongholds has to start in your mind. When a person has dealt well with their own thought life, they become positioned to recognize those strongholds in others—not to bring shame, but to bring victory through prayer. We praise who God is, aligning ourselves internally first, which empowers us to release that knowledge of God into the world. Winning battles internally positions us to influence the world externally.

Prepare your hearts and minds for action! Stay alert and fix your hope firmly on the marvelous grace that is coming to you. For when Jesus Christ is unveiled, a greater measure of grace will be released to you. I PETER 1:13 TPT

***

Has the enemy tried to attack your thought life with fear, doubt, or anxiety? What areas seem particularly susceptible to his lies? How can you strengthen these areas by connecting with God and hearing His truth for your life?

OTHER SIDE OF THE STORM

"I will show my greatness and my holiness, and I will make myself known in the sight of many nations. Then they will know that I am the LORD."
EZEKIEL 38:23 NIV

I will speak to the storms in my life and say, "Be removed!"

Jonah's storm came when he was trying to flee from God's assignment. When the disciples faced the storm, they were following God's instructions, trying to cross to the other side. The storm they hit was an obstacle to the will of God. Jesus had taught them what to do with obstacles. If there was a mountain in their way, they were to speak to the mountain and say, "Go, throw yourself into the sea" (Mark 11:23).

Obstacles to the will of God are to be dealt with as though we are dealing with the enemy himself. Jesus napped in the boat while the storm raged around them. Jesus trusted His disciples to deal with the obstacle in the authority He had given them. This was a missed opportunity for them to step into the peace of God, taking authority over the storm.

When the storm calmed, the disciples and Jesus arrived at the other side and met a demon-possessed man. As soon as he saw Jesus, he fell down at His feet and worshipped Him. Jesus cast the demons out of him and into a herd of pigs. The people of that area were so afraid when they heard, they asked Jesus to leave. The newly freed man became an evangelist to his town, and the Bible says when Jesus returned to that region, great multitudes came out to see Him and be healed (see Matthew 15:30). There was radical transformation not only in that one man but in the entire community.

When the disciples were facing the storm, they weren't aware that God was setting them up to touch one person whose deliverance would break a territorial spirit and set an entire region free to come to Christ. On the other side of the storm was tremendous victory.

God will use the storms we face to strengthen us, but the storm itself is there for a reason: to keep us from the breakthrough that could potentially shake an entire nation. We can speak to those storms and say, "Be removed!"

All glory to God, who is able to make you strong, just as my Good News says. This message about Jesus Christ has revealed his plan for you Gentiles, a plan kept secret from the beginning of time. But now as the prophets foretold and

as the eternal God has commanded, this message is made known to all Gentiles everywhere, so that they too might believe and obey him.
ROMANS 16:25-26 NLT

***

What kind of storm are you facing? Is it like Jonah's, trying to get you to flee from God's call on your life? Or, is it like the one the disciples faced—a clear attack from the enemy, attempting to prevent them from seeing God's will be done? If it is the latter, stand in the peace of God and tell that storm to "Be removed in the name of Jesus!"

A SUPERIOR TRUTH

"Our Beloved Father, dwelling in the heavenly realms, may the glory of your name be the center on which our lives turn. Manifest your kingdom realm, and cause your every purpose to be fulfilled on earth, just as it is in heaven."
MATTHEW 6:9-10 TPT

If it's not in heaven, God doesn't want it on the earth.

Not all truth is created equal. Throughout Scripture, there are revelations of truth that are then amended by a superior truth. For example, the entire Old Testament was focused on building a consciousness in mankind that they were sinners in need of God. The revelation that they received was the real power of sin. It was illustrated in the fact that in the Old Testament if you touched a leper, you became unclean (see Leviticus 13).

In the New Testament, the love of God triumphs over the power of sin. It is a superior revelation. Jesus touched the leper and, instead of Jesus becoming unclean, the leper became clean (see Matthew 8:3). The New Testament as a whole introduces a superior revelation of truth: The Old Testament had the law, and the law was perfect. But the New Testament has grace; it is superior. Judgment is a real issue, but mercy triumphs over judgment (see James 2:13). Sin is powerful, but love covers a multitude of sins (see 1 Peter 4:8).

Jesus is the exact representation of the Father's nature (see John 14:9). He was *exactly* representing the Father's nature when He reached into the mud and wiped it in the blind man's eyes to heal him (see John 9:6). He was illustrating the Father's heart when He raised the dead child in front of her grieving family (see Mark 5). In every way, the person of Jesus illustrated the heart of the Father.

Many people believe that the Father brings bad things into their lives—illness, poverty, torment—in order to teach them a lesson or develop their character. They imagine, then, that Jesus contends with the Father for our release from suffering. But this is a blasphemous lie. Everything Jesus did was to reveal the Father's nature to the world. If it's not in heaven, God doesn't want it on the earth.

> "I have come down from heaven, not to do my own will but the will of him who sent me."
> JOHN 6:38 ESV

***

What aspects of Jesus' life challenge your understanding of the Father? Are there any

assumptions you've made of the Father's nature, because of the challenges in your life, that you need to change? Invite the Father to reveal His heart to you today.

LIVING WITH MYSTERY

Bless the LORD, my soul, And all that is within me, bless His holy name. Bless the LORD, my soul, And do not forget any of His benefits; Who pardons all your guilt, Who heals all your diseases; Who redeems your life from the pit, Who crowns you with favor and compassion; Who satisfies your years with good things, So that your youth is renewed like the eagle.
PSALM 103:1-5 NASB

The more I trust Him in mystery, the more He can trust me with what I can understand.

In the first few verses of Psalm 103, David commands his soul—his emotions, mind, and will—to come into alignment with who God is. He tells himself not to forget who God is, knowing that life gives all of us plenty of opportunity to forget.

We do not have a complicated gospel. We don't have to guess about the nature of God or His will for the earth. This gospel we embrace and live by is filled with absolutes about who God is. But we live in the tension between that which we understand and the realm called *mystery*. The Christian life is a combination of the two. Proverbs encourages us to seek understanding, but we cannot afford to only live in what we understand (see Proverbs 4).

If we restrict our walk in this way, we are limiting ourselves to traveling the same familiar roads we've always traveled. We do not grow in our relationship with the Lord unless we expose ourselves to impossibilities that force us to have questions that we cannot answer. That's why the Christian life is called the faith. We don't need faith for the familiar. Trust implies "I do not understand." Our ability to live with a combination of knowing God's nature through revelation and trusting Him in all that we do not understand defines the true Christian life.

Sometimes we want answers so badly we begin to invent answers that make us feel good about our present condition. But, to do it, we have to take one of the absolutes that God has revealed to us about His nature—God is good, His desire is that all should be saved, He paid the price for every sin and every illness—and we have to sacrifice it on the altar of human reasoning.

The more we trust Him in the mystery, all that we cannot understand, the more He can trust us with the revelation knowledge we can understand.

Through the revelation of the Anointed One, he
  unveiled his secret desires to us—the hidden
  mystery of his long-range plan, which he was

delighted to implement from the very beginning of time.
EPHESIANS 1:9 TPT

***

What mystery are you facing right now? List the things you don't understand about your situation. Now list the absolutes of God's nature that you know to be true.

EYES ON GOD

Those who look to him are radiant; their faces are never covered with shame. This poor man called, and the LORD heard him; he saved him out of all his troubles. The angel of the LORD encamps around those who fear him, and he delivers them. Taste and see that the LORD is good; blessed is the one who takes refuge in him.
PSALM 34:5-8 NIV

Delayed breakthrough can fuel my prayers, but courage is found in focusing on Him.

Rest is always an inside job. We could have the most boring schedules in the world and still be filled with anxiety and stress. True rest comes from learning how to live from the presence of God, keeping our eyes on Him and what He is doing. That is our connection, our lifeline, to the peace found in God's presence.

John the Baptist was the greatest man to have ever been born prior to Jesus (see Matthew 11:11), but even John had a moment of doubt. Sitting in prison, he sent out a message for Jesus, "Are you the one who is to come, or should we expect someone else?" (11:3) That question had already been answered. It had been answered at Jesus' water baptism and by John himself when he proclaimed, "Look, the Lamb of God...!" (John 1:29) He already knew who Jesus was, but in the midst of crisis, his peace was shaken and doubts flooded in.

It's easy to question our previously held beliefs when we're in trouble or experiencing disappointment. John the Baptist was locked in prison because he had prepared the way for the One who sets the captives free (see Isaiah 61:1). He was living in the tension and mystery of seeing God fulfill His promise to the world without experiencing that same breakthrough for himself. Jesus didn't get mad at him for questioning though. He responded, "Go and report back to John what you hear and see: The blind receive sight, the lame walk, those who have leprosy are cleansed, the deaf hear, the dead are raised, and the good news is proclaimed to the poor" (Matthew 11:4-5).

John's attention had been diverted away from God and onto the very real danger he was facing. Jesus simply took his face between His hands and redirected his focus back onto what God was doing. Delayed breakthrough can fuel our prayers, but courage is found in focusing on Him. Behold, as the eyes of servants look to the hand of their masters, As the eyes of a maid to the hand of her mistress, So our eyes look to the LORD our God, Until He has mercy on us.

PSALM 123:2 NKJV

***

Begin to make a list of what you *do* see God doing in your life and in the world around you. How can you see His nature being revealed on the earth even if you haven't experienced personal breakthrough yet?

SUPERNATURAL COURAGE

"Be strong and courageous, do not be afraid or in dread of them, for the LORD your God is the One who is going with you. He will not desert you or abandon you."
DEUTERONOMY 31:6 NASB

My boldness will release a sense of identity and purpose into people around me.

The book of Samuel tells an astounding story of powerful, supernatural courage. Jonathan stood with his armor-bearer looking at a whole troop of the enemy Philistine army. In so many words, he says, "I think we can take them." And the armor-bearer—the real hero of the story—looked at their odds and said, "Yeah, let's do it. I'm with you!" The two men gave up every military advantage, climbing uphill toward the enemy in plain sight, and still the Philistines "fell before Jonathan" (1 Samuel 14:13). The earth itself shook, announcing the victory.

Then something extraordinary happened: the Bible says that the Hebrew people, the ones who had turned so far from God they were fighting with the enemy, heard the story of the two men's supernatural courage, and they could no longer deny who they were (see 1 Samuel 14:21). Imagine them taking off the Philistine military gear, leaving formation, and running to join their Hebrew brothers and sisters in battle. Supernatural courage causes people to discover their identity.

It also brings heroes out of hiding. Men of Israel who had been hiding from the battle in the mountains now ran to the frontlines (see 1 Samuel 14:22). They hadn't gone as far as to join the Philistines, but they hadn't yet discovered their purpose for living. Somehow, the story of supernatural courage reached the caves where they'd cowered, and they could no longer stay hidden. They ran and began to chase after the very ones who had so terrified them.

In every battle, we have the opportunity to be Jonathan and his armor-bearer, seeing the situation through the eyes of God—the One who is not intimidated, the One about whom we can say with confidence: "The Lord is not limited to saving by many or by few" (1 Samuel 14:6). In every crisis we have the chance to see our acts of boldness release a sense of identity and purpose into the people around us.

Remember to stay alert and hold firmly to all that you believe. Be mighty and full of courage.
1 CORINTHIANS 16:13 TPT

***

Who in your life has turned so far from the things of God that they are fighting with the enemy now? Who are those who, while they haven't left God, are hiding and disengaged? Ask the Lord to stir up your heart of boldness. Cry out to God that your courage would awaken the hearts of those individuals!

SHELTERED IN HIS GOODNESS

The LORD is good, A stronghold in the day of trouble, And He knows those who take refuge in Him.
NAHUM 1:7 NASB

Nothing sits outside of the scope of God's redemption.

God is not uncomfortable with our pain and sorrow. Jesus wept at the death of His friend, Lazarus, even though He knew He was about to raise him from the dead (see John 11:35). Often we are not meant to feel sad without taking action. God has given us the ability to feel so that our emotions will take us back to Him.

If we feel grief, pain, or trouble, we can let those emotions take us to Him in prayer. Even if we don't know exactly how to pray for a situation, we do know that if there has been destruction, death, or joy stolen from us, the enemy has had his way. And we know that we can take a stand against the kingdom of darkness, praying for God's mercy to touch that circumstance. Emotion is a gift; we perceive because He has positioned us to make a difference through prayer.

If we find ourselves sinking into hopelessness, we are falling into the lie of believing that there are certain things outside of God's reach. Instead, we can run into the reality of Jesus, taking shelter in His name and in His goodness. Then, we can begin to see the situation before us through His eyes, thinking the redemptive solutions that He is thinking.

In Scripture, the idea of a stronghold most often refers to a place of demonic residence in the life of an individual or a city. But, in the case of Nahum, the stronghold is a revelation of the goodness of God. Proverbs says it this way, "The name of the LORD is a strong tower; the righteous runs into it and is safe" (Proverbs 18:10).

Picture it like this: people who truly understand the goodness of God automatically have a hiding place, a stronghold in which they dwell no matter the storm. When we are faced with problems, we can run toward God's goodness to find shelter. We can take refuge in the knowledge that He always has a solution. Nothing sits outside of the scope of God's redemption.

You are my hiding place; You, LORD, protect me from trouble; You surround me with songs and shouts of deliverance.
PSALM 32:7 AMP

***

Make a list of testimonies of God's goodness that you have witnessed in your own life, in the lives of friends or family, and even in the stories of the Bible. Tape this list somewhere you can see it daily, reviewing the reality of God's goodness whenever you feel hopeless. He is your hiding place.

THE POWER OF TRUST

> Trust in the LORD with all your heart, And lean not on your own understanding.
> PROVERBS 3:5 NKJV

The strength of my heart comes from my complete abandonment to the purposes of God.

Your heart is bigger than your head. What can be grasped by the heart of man is so much more significant that what can be fathomed by the mind. The mind is not insignificant; it is important. But the Bible makes it clear that our minds are not to be in control (see 2 Corinthians 10:5). Small-minded people are actually people who put their mind first. If the mind is chief, we will reduce our walk with God to only what we can understand.

It's important that we have parts of our lives that are buried in mystery. Mystery is as important as revelation. In our quest to know God, to serve Him, and to illustrate His kingdom to the world, we will gain understanding. That which we didn't understand in our early walk with God, we may understand now. That's how it is supposed to be; we increase in our revelation of Him.

As we progress in our understanding of the kingdom, so we must progress in our acceptance of mystery. We need to always have enough of what we can neither explain nor control in our lives because that is what gives us reasons to trust.

In the Proverb above, the word *lean* refers to depending on something for support. If you lean on a table, you are trusting the weight of your body to that table; if it weren't there, you'd fall over. It is supporting you. Proverbs is telling us not to let our own understanding be that which supports us through our life.

As our understanding of our faith increases, we need to take more risk, staying exposed to need in such a way that it becomes normal for us to lean not on our own understanding, but in all of our ways acknowledge God. Our personal insight cannot be the source of our strength. The strength of our hearts comes from our complete abandonment to the purposes of God.

The secret things belong to the LORD our God, but the things which are revealed and disclosed belong to us and to our children forever, so that we may do all of the words of this law.
DEUTERONOMY 29:29 AMP

***

What are some of the ways you have grown in your understanding of God since you first started following Him? What felt

confusing about your walk with the Lord previously that is no longer confusing? How are you actively taking risk, keeping mystery in your life with Him?

FROM OUR KNEES

"If My people who are called by My name will humble themselves, and pray and seek My face, and turn from their wicked ways, then I will hear from heaven, and will forgive their sin and heal their land."
2 CHRONICLES 7:14 NKJV

If I am to represent God in my actions, I must first encounter Him in my prayers.

The Lord places the weight of responsibility of transforming the world on the shoulders of His people. God has a habit of bringing healing and restoration, but it is instigated by the people with whom He has shared His name. Jesus said, "Whatever you ask the Father in My name He will give you" (John 16:23), and "If two of you agree on earth concerning anything that they ask, it will be done for them by My Father in heaven. For where two or three are gathered together in My name, I am there in the midst of them" (Matthew 18:19-20).

The weight of responsibility for the transformational expressions of God's kingdom rests on the shoulders of those to whom He has given His name. We are not here on earth taking up space, keeping busy until we die or

Jesus returns. We are here tasked with changing the world: on earth as it is in heaven.

Worship and prayer are the primary assignments we've been given. It's from our knees that we have the greatest impact on the world around us. It's from the place of intercession that we become actual partners with God. He's not looking for people who know how to stay busy; He's looking for people who know how to represent His heart. It's the connection with the heart of God that gives us the authority to represent Him to the world with absolute confidence.

We've been called to a lifestyle of prayer. Cultivating our awareness of the presence of God with us and upon us is that which makes the difference to the world around us. God looks for partnership. To paraphrase St. Augustine, "Without Him, we can't; without us, He won't."

As we come into a place of agreement with the heart and mind of God, we are able to exercise His authority, that His will would be done here as it is in heaven. If we are to represent Him in our actions, we must first encounter Him in our prayers.

"Call to Me and I will answer you, and tell you [and even show you] great and mighty things, [things which have been confined and hidden], which you do not know and understand and cannot distinguish."

JEREMIAH 33:3 AMP

85

***

What has been stirring your heart in prayer lately? Spend some time with the Lord to hear His heart about that issue. How can you partner with Him in prayer and worship?

CONTENDING VS RESTING

"From the days of John the Baptist until now the kingdom of heaven suffers violence, and the violent take it by force."
MATTHEW 11:12 NKJV

God made me for relationship, and that is the only way forward.

There are two different ways that we see faith described in the Bible. The first is a violent warfare where we take the spiritual weapons we have—our prophetic words, the Word of God, bold declarations, prophetic acts—and wage war on anything standing in the way of our breakthrough. The other way is entirely different. We are called to rest and receive our breakthrough with the trust and surrender of children. We sit back and watch our triumph unfold (see 2 Chronicles 20:17).

Whenever the Lord is highlighting a season where we are to obtain breakthrough through the violence of faith, it's because He's wanting us to learn our authority in Him. When He wants us to be still and receive by faith like a child, He's teaching us about our identity as a son or daughter of God.

Sometimes, He is intentionally showing us how to use the authority that He has entrusted into our hands. And then, perhaps the very next week, He wants us to inhabit a place of rest. In those moments, we could try to fight for breakthrough—confessing, declaring, marching, fasting, waving our flags, shaking our tambourines, and blowing the shofars. But, until we discover who we are and rest in that identity, nothing will be released to us.

How do we know what season we're in? We would all love for there to be a recipe for faith. There are times when we don't know if we're supposed to come out swinging in the face of opposition or if we're supposed to sit back and wait. But we will never step into this understanding out of a principle; we'll only step into it out of a relationship. Often, we try to reduce things of the kingdom to a concept instead of a journey with the Father. Whether we are to contend or rest, He made us for relationship, and that is the only way forward.

> Then Jesus called for the children and said to the disciples, "Let the children come to me.
> Don't stop them! For the Kingdom of God belongs to those who are like these children."
> LUKE 18:16 NLT

***

Think back over your history with God. Do you remember times when the breakthrough came after warlike contending on the part of you and those you love? Have you experienced seasons when God is wanting you to sit back and simply receive from Him? How did you know the difference?

ABANDONING INTROSPECTION

> We know how much God loves us, and we have put our trust in his love. God is love, and all who live in love live in God, and God lives in them.
> I JOHN 4:16 NLT

God is in a good mood!

Sometimes, when we want to see God's will on the earth, when we want to make sure our hearts are pure before Him, we can fall into the trap of introspection. With all good intentions, we mistakenly think that if we only examine our motives closely enough, we can somehow transform ourselves.

As a younger pastor, when I took myself too seriously, I would become harsh and hard because I wanted to see transformation so badly. If I wasn't seeing certain miracles, I would conclude that there must be sin in my life that I just couldn't see. I would dive deep in introspection to find it.

I placed so much effort into being "spiritual" and effective, straining against every weakness in myself. I would examine my own motives constantly, trying to find anything I could to fix. It was killing me, so I decided that I had to stop. The seasons in my life when I was the healthiest were the seasons I was relaxed, enjoying life in God and ministry.

Introspection is damaging. It takes away our confidence in the only One who brings true transformation. We begin to put too much weight on our own role. We do have a role in transforming our lives—we need to remain humble, teachable, surrendered—but His role is so much greater.

So, we can pray this instead: "God, I read the Bible every day, and You said Your Word is sharper than a two-edged sword. I'm with Your people all the time. Give me the slap of a friend if there's something I need to see in my heart. I welcome the correction. I'm in Your presence constantly, and Your presence is a burning fire. Burn away anything that is not of You. I'm going to quit looking internally to find something wrong with me. I will assume all is well until You say otherwise."

God is not distant. He doesn't wait until we're perfect to embrace us. He is not mad at us. God is in a good mood!

> The Lord is not slow in keeping his promise, as some understand slowness. Instead he is patient with you, not wanting anyone to perish, but everyone to come to repentance.
> 2 PETER 3:9 NIV

***

Have you ever fallen into the trap of introspection? What was the fruit of that season? Are you open to correction coming in the ways mentioned in the prayer above? Can you trust that God will bring correction to you if you need it?

FAMILY FIRST

"A new command I give you: Love one another. As I have loved you, so you must love one another. By this everyone will know that you are my disciples, if you love one another."
JOHN 13:34-35 NIV

My compassion for others will silence the voice of the storm.

In Nehemiah, the people of God were in trouble (see Nehemiah 5). There was a famine. They had no crops to harvest, and they were running out of money. In an attempt to survive, some people were selling their own children into slavery. Others were selling off their family land. This land was meant to be the God-given, permanent inheritance of individual family lines. To sell their children and their land would have impacted their legacy forever.

When Nehemiah heard the cries of the starving people, he quickly saw the root of the problem: the wealthier Israelites were loaning money to their countrymen with steep interest rates. The purpose of loaning money to their fellow Israelites was to help one another, so charging interest had been forbidden (see Deuteronomy 23:19-20). It was particularly egregious to do so in the midst of a famine. People weren't able to keep up with the payments and were losing their inheritance from God. Nehemiah rebuked the Israelites, calling them back to their national covenant and their focus on family.

The spirit of division and self-preservation, so present during challenging times, was counteracted by Nehemiah's focus on mercy and on the restoration of relationships. This was no time to take advantage of one another; it was time to pull together as a supportive community. They would weather the storm together.

During times of crisis, it can be tempting for us to withdraw and become preoccupied with our own needs. Instead, God would have us see the opportunity before us to aggressively pursue love for our neighbors. Instead of reacting to the fear of the day, we are to refine our focus on our practical, simple devotion to Christ and His people.

Our love for God should be seen and measured by our love for others. The famine in Nehemiah happened, but we never hear of it spoken again in Scripture. It's as though their compassion for each other, their devotion to one another, silenced the voice of that storm.

It is absolutely clear that God has called you to a free life. Just make sure that you don't use this freedom as an excuse to do whatever you want to do and destroy your freedom. Rather,

use your freedom to serve one another in love; that's how freedom grows. For everything we know about God's Word is summed up in a single sentence: Love others as you love yourself. That's an act of true freedom.
GALATIANS 5:13-14 MSG

***

How have you experienced the spirit of division or self-preservation trying to impact you during times of conflict? How could you stir yourself with compassion for others even in the face of your own need? What is one act of practical love you could show someone in your community today?

CONFESS AND DECLARE

"The Spirit of the LORD is upon Me, Because He has anointed Me To preach the gospel to the poor; He has sent Me to heal the brokenhearted, To proclaim liberty to the captives And recovery of sight to the blind, To set at liberty those who are oppressed."
LUKE 4:18 NKJV

With bold declarations of trust in God, I infuse hope into others.

"I will say of the LORD, 'He is my refuge and my fortress; My God, in Him I will trust'" (Psalm 91:2). In the past, I have taken this verse and turned it into a personal declaration. I would say, "God, You are the One I trust. You are my refuge." But then it hit me one day; the psalmist chose that specific wording for a reason.

We are supposed to confess and declare that He is the One we trust. This is important to speak out over our lives. In this verse, these are actually confessions and declarations that we are meant to make to one another. "I will say of the LORD..." We are to guard our tongues, speaking life and hope to one another especially when times are difficult.

Both hopelessness and hope are contagious. We get to choose how infectious we want to be and with what we infect others. In Isaiah 35:4, it says, "Say to those who are fearful-hearted, 'Be strong, do not fear!'"

If someone is experiencing fear or struggling with hopelessness, we don't shame them. We can throw one another a lifeline by intentionally anchoring our hearts and words in hope. Words of life, confessed over one another, have deep impact. The very next verse in Isaiah explains the effect of the previous encouragement: "Then the eyes of the blind shall be opened, and the ears of the deaf shall be unstopped" (Isaiah 35:5).

Intentional words, spoken over ourselves and one another, have the power to bring hope, strength, healing, and supernatural courage. We declare what God has said and done, instead of fueling an atmosphere of fear that tries to grip people's hearts. In this way, we hold up one another's arms—as Aaron did for Moses—in the midst of the battle (see Exodus 17:12). We remind one another of who God is, what He has done, and where our trust lies. With bold declarations of trust in God, we infuse hope into one another.

You are a chosen race, a royal priesthood, a consecrated nation, a [special] people for God's own possession, so that you may proclaim the excellencies [the wonderful deeds and virtues and perfections] of Him who called you out of darkness into His marvelous light. I PETER 2:9 AMP

***

Think back over your life. Who held your arms up in the middle of your battles? What things did they say or do that brought courage and healing to you? How could you show up in that same way for others?

THE FATHER OF FAITH

Our light and momentary trouble are achieving for us an eternal glory that far outweighs them all. So we fix our eyes not on what is seen, but on what is unseen, since what is seen is temporary, but what is unseen is eternal.
2 CORINTHIANS 4:17-18 NIV

Hope is the atmosphere through which impossibility is released into the earth; it redefines my circumstances.

The heart of the Lord for every single person is that they would step fully into their destinies. The Lord said that Abraham would be a father of nations and Abraham took that word and let it redefine his world. He looked at his 100-year-old body and his 90-year-old wife who'd dealt with years of infertility, and he chose to stand firm on the promises of God. In that atmosphere of contagious hope, a miracle came forth, and he became the father of nations.

Abraham's nephew, Lot, on the other hand, became overwhelmed by the sinful conduct of people around him (see 2 Peter 2:7). Because of this, his own effectiveness was crippled. Abraham defined his surroundings; Lot was defined by his surroundings. Both men are called righteous, both will spend eternity with God, and both had promises from God over their lives. The primary difference between the two was their level of hope.

The Bible says, "Against all hope, Abraham in hope believed and so became the father of many nations" (Romans 4:18). We don't know much about Lot's descendants, but Abraham's legacy is renowned. Infectious hope—the kind that defines our circumstances—creates the atmosphere for legacy.

Hebrews says it is by faith we inherit promises (6:12). This verse doesn't mean that faith helps us to have fulfilled promises. Rather, it means that abiding faith actually attracts promises from God that you wouldn't get otherwise. God is a good steward; He plants in healthy environments. In the kingdom, a healthy environment is the heart of hope.

It's hard to keep natural hope alive. If that were all we had, we would have to constantly work to force ourselves to feel positive about negative situations. When you have a word from God, holding onto that word becomes a life source. God wants to birth certain things on the earth for His glory. Hope becomes the womb from which a legacy is born. It is the atmosphere through which impossibility is released into the earth; it redefines our circumstances.

"Fear not, for I have redeemed you; I have called you by name, you are mine. When you pass

through the waters, I will be with you; and through the rivers, they shall not overwhelm you; when you walk through fire you shall not be burned, and the flame shall not consume you."
ISAIAH 43:1-2 ESV

***

What promises have you received from God about your family, your community, and your future? What circumstances are trying to distract you from God's word over your life? How can your understanding of God's goodness and faithfulness begin to redefine your surroundings?

WORSHIP OR WORRY

"I hold this against you: You have forsaken the love you had at first. Consider how far you have fallen! Repent and do the things you did at first."
REVELATION 2:4-5 NIV

Being a worshipper is what positions me to pray effectively.

We've probably all had those nights when we can't sleep, when our minds keep turning over an issue, and rest feels far away. In those moments, our anxiety can dominate our awareness of God, turning our prayers into worries or complaints. Our affection and adoration for God, for Jesus, for the Holy Spirit is at the core of who we are. When we can return to the place of affection, our hearts burning for Him, it changes everything.

Solomon noted, "I slept but my heart was awake" (Song of Songs 5:2). A number of years ago, I learned to turn my heart of affection toward the Lord as I was falling asleep at night. In those moments, I would engage with Him and sense His presence. After trying this for a while, I realized that most people would have much better days if they had better nights.

In Genesis, it says of creation, "And there was evening, and there was morning—the first day" (1:5). Biblically, our day actually begins the night before. As I learned to turn my affection toward Him each evening, resting in that place of presence, an incredible peace would come over me, making it easy to sleep. Even if I woke up in the middle of the night, I could simply turn my heart of affection back toward Him.

One particular night, I didn't do this practice of affection. Instead of turning my heart toward Him, I wrestled with an issue in my mind until I couldn't fall back asleep. When I got up in the morning, I felt like the Lord said, "Worry replaced worship."

As a son of God, I sit at a table of worship. That night, I had chosen to give a seat to fear, anxiety, and worry. I needed to reposition myself, returning to the place of worship in His presence that had become my home. Being a worshipper (not a worrier) is what positions me to pray effectively.

Set your mind and keep focused habitually on the things above [the heavenly things], not on things that are on the earth [which have only temporal value].

COLOSSIANS 3:2 AMP

***

What is your routine before going to bed? What thoughts fill your mind as you fall asleep? How could you intentionally focus

on your affection for God every evening, experiencing His peaceful presence.

GATES OF PRAISE

"Violence shall no longer be heard in your land, Neither wasting nor destruction within your borders; But you shall call your walls Salvation, And your gates Praise."
ISAIAH 60:18 NKJV

Jesus came to give me life.

Isaiah 60 gives us a profound picture of the spiritual city of Zion. Around this city are walls called Salvation with gates of Praise. In Revelation, the gates were made out of one solid pearl (see Revelation 21:21). A pearl is formed through irritation and conflict. The conflict for us, as believers, is that we live with the tension of knowing that God is absolutely good all of the time while we experience circumstances that are anything but good.

When we can praise Him within this conflict, without knowing all the answers, without manipulation or redefining His nature, when we can praise Him by truly exalting His nature, these are the moments of sacrificial praise. It is within this sacrifice, that the pearl—the gate from Isaiah 60—is formed.

A gate is a place of access. Our gates of praise are where the King of Glory enters to invade a situation. Many people have acquired the walls of salvation, but they have no entrance point for God to invade because they haven't been able to praise in the middle of a circumstance they don't understand.

In Psalms, it says, "The LORD loves the gates of Zion more than all the dwellings of Jacob" (Psalm 87:2). How could a gate be compared to a dwelling place? In this context, the gate of praise is where His presence rests. The gate is where the King dwells. The gate is formed by moving above our human reasoning, above demanding an explanation for a problem, and into a place of deep trust. In the midst of what we cannot explain, we hold onto the truth that He is good all the time. The devourer would have you redefine God through the lens of your circumstance, but God is not the devourer. Jesus came to give life.

> Why do you remain distant, refusing to answer my tearful cries in the day and my desperate cries for your help in the night? I can't stop sobbing. Where are you, my God? Yet I know that you are most holy. You are God-Enthroned, the praise of Israel.
> PSALM 22:2-3 TPT

***

Where are the gates of praise in your life? Take some time to remember the

moments in your history with God when you have offered Him a sacrifice of praise. Picture those places now as gates where His presence can rush in to transform your life.

CONTINUAL DEVOTION

"You shall love the LORD your God with all your heart, and with all your soul (life), and with all your mind (thought, understanding), and with all your strength."
MARK 12:30 AMP

God will set me on high, delivering me from any kind of trouble.

There's an old joke about a married couple who visit a counselor to work on their relationship. The wife is upset because her husband never says that he loves her. Exasperated, the husband responds, "I told her I loved her on our wedding day, and nothing has changed since then!"

It's funny only because we know that love doesn't work like that. When we're married, we declare our love for our spouses often, sometimes many times a day. We don't repeat our love because anything has changed or we're worried our spouse may have forgotten. It's a chance for us to frequently re-set our focus on our covenant of love.

The Lord values this kind of continual devotion. The Bible says, "Because he has set his love on Me, therefore I will save him; I will set him [securely] on high, because he knows My name" (Psalm 91:14). God invites us to fix the affection of our hearts on Him, learning how to anchor ourselves continuously in our devotion to Him.

In Acts 2 it says that the disciples were "continually and faithfully devoting themselves to the instruction of the apostles, and to fellowship, to eating meals together and to prayers" (verse 42). Despite the persecution happening to believers, they continually devoted themselves to their covenant with God, and from that, they saw incredible fruit.

There's something about the ongoing, re-setting of our affection on God throughout the day. He's such a lover that He is drawn to our affection. He responds with His presence and His covering.

When we go through difficult situations, we can stop and turn our affection toward Him until we can sense His presence resting on us. Whether He shows up in a new way or we become more aware of His presence, intentionally setting our love on Him changes something. We know His name. He will set us on high, delivering us from any kind of trouble.

Love the LORD, all His godly ones! The LORD watches over the faithful But fully repays the one who acts arrogantly.
PSALM 31:23 NASB

***

How could you develop this as a practice in your daily life? Whether it is setting a reminder on your phone or placing notes for yourself around the house, think of a way to practice turning your affection to the Lord continuously throughout your day. How do you experience His presence when you do this? What is the fruit of this intentional practice?

FRUITFULNESS IN PRAISE

The LORD is my strength and my song, and he has become my salvation; this is my God, and I will praise him, my father's God, and I will exalt him.
EXODUS 15:2 ESV

I will look to God as my deliverer, and nothing will sway me.

In Hebrew, Judah means "praise" and Ephraim means "fruitful, fertile, productive." In the book of Zechariah, God joins together the idea of fruitfulness in partnership with praise. He says, "For I have bent Judah as my bow; I have made Ephraim its arrow... and wield you like a warrior's sword" (9:13). Praise is where strength is found.

Let's say we hear some distressing news, have a conflict with a friend, get a bad report from a doctor, or we experience a career disappointment. In the middle of it, we can stop and choose to give the sacrifice of praise that brings forth fruitfulness in our lives. We can acknowledge that He is God, that He is on the throne, and that nothing is outside of His notice or care. All of the promises of His Word belong to us, and we can give Him honor in the midst of our pain. Even though we may not know how everything will work out, we can give Him an offering of our trust.

The Bible calls that offering *strength*; it calls that choice *fruitfulness*. Even though we may not feel like it, when we acknowledge God's sovereignty—His rule over every situation—we are engaging in the battle of life. Our hearts are not focused on the problems; they are focused on Him. We release the problems into His hands, trusting that He will bring the solution.

In the next chapter of Zechariah, the prophet says that Judah will become like a "majestic steed in battle" (10:3). Horses used in war are not afraid of conflict; they charge into the fray. When there's difficulty around them, they hold their focus. This is how the Lord describes His worshiping people.

He said we will become as warhorses. We will hear the Word of the Lord and, regardless of what is happening around us, we will not be shaken. We are confident in who God is and what He has promised us. We look to Him as our deliverer, and nothing will sway us.

> Shout in celebration of praise to the Lord! Everyone who loves the Lord and delights in him ... They will not live in fear or dread of what may come, for their hearts are firm, ever secure in their faith. Steady and strong, they will not

be afraid, but will calmly face their every foe until they all go down in defeat.
PSALM 112:1, 7-8 TPT

***

Are you aware of God's sovereignty as you engage with your battle? How can you turn your attention from focusing on the problem at hand to focusing on the One who will deliver you?

WINDS OF ADVERSITY

"Yahweh will always guide you where to go and what to do. He will fill you with refreshment even when you are in a dry, difficult place. He will continually restore strength to you, so you will flourish like a well-watered garden and like an ever-flowing, trustworthy spring of blessing."
ISAIAH 58:11 TPT

Everything about me was perfectly designed to demonstrate God to the world.

Both favor and trial drive us somewhere. We are like sailboats; where the winds of adversity and blessing drive us is determined by how we handle the sail and the rudder of our hearts. Both experiences are designed to push us deeper into God.

Monitoring our hearts—our value systems, attitudes, and confessions—is the way we set the rudder and the sail. Favor and trial are both able to take us toward becoming the best example of Jesus we can possibly be. However, if our rudder is set wrong, favor can move us into self-promotion, and trial can send us into self-pity.

One of the best examples of this is in the life of Solomon. He had possibly the most unusual level of favor ever seen on the earth.

Favor was meant to drive him into becoming all he was designed to be—a perfect, complete representation of the heart and nature of God. But something entered his heart that distorted the divine purpose on his life. King Solomon loved many foreign women (see 1 Kings 11:1). He married foreign women in an attempt to curry favor with those kingdoms. Instead of leaning on the Lord, he tried to obtain through self-promotion what had already been given to him by God.

Winds of adversity present us with a choice. We can either lean into fear—violating our design—or trust that every moment has been divinely orchestrated that we might illustrate the victory of Christ in a given situation.

Jesus Christ was raised from the dead. He doesn't need our choices to validate that miracle. But, when we pray for the sick and they are healed, it's a demonstration of the resurrection power of Jesus. When we defeat a personal addiction, that's a demonstration of His resurrection power. When we face a mental battle and resolve to obey the Lord no matter what until we experience lasting victory, we're demonstrating the resurrection power of Jesus. Everything about us was perfectly designed to demonstrate Him to the world.

It is by grace [God's remarkable compassion and favor drawing you to Christ] that you have been saved [actually delivered from judgment and given

eternal life] through faith. And this [salvation] is not of yourselves [not through your own effort], but it is the [undeserved, gracious] gift of God; not as a result of [your] works [nor your attempts to keep the Law], so that no one will [be able to] boast or take credit in any way [for his salvation].
EPHESIANS 2:8-9 AMP

✳✳✳

In what direction have the winds of favor sent you? What about the winds of trial? How can you position the rudder and sail of your heart in trust, thankfulness, and worship so that—no matter what—those winds push you deeper into God?

FAITH-FILLED HEART

A wise person scales the city of the mighty And brings down the stronghold in which they trust.
PROVERBS 21:22 NASB

Bold faith stands on the shoulders of quiet trust.

Proverbs 21:22 gives incredible insight into strategies for seeing family lines, cities, and nations transformed. A walled city would have been inaccessible to an individual, but in this verse, the man's wisdom allows him to destroy a stronghold of trust. God's target throughout Scripture is our trust in Him. It's central to our relationship with Him, as "without faith it is impossible to please Him" (Hebrews 11:6). The Bible doesn't say without worship, without prayer, or even without reading the Bible. These are all essential parts of our walk with the Lord, but the verse says "without faith."

God is the most trustworthy individual in the universe, and it is a violation of creation to not trust the One who is worthy of trust. Our trust is a debt that we owe Him. We are obligated to reflect His faithfulness through our trust. Strongholds, in this sense, are whatever we trust in other than God. These strongholds become particularly evident when we are in trouble.

When we're in distress, whatever we reach for—other than God—has taken His place. For some it's sports, achievement, substance abuse, or even recreational activities. Some of these things are wonderful additions to our lives, but when they become the thing we turn to in trouble, they have usurped our dependency on the Lord. When that is the case, we may declare our belief in the existence of God, but our lifestyle testifies otherwise.

When Jesus told the rich, young ruler, "Sell your possessions and give to the poor," it wasn't an issue of money, it was an issue of trust (see Matthew 19:21). He had to sell everything to follow Jesus. We know that Mary, Martha, and Lazarus were very wealthy, and Jesus never told them to give their wealth away. How much money is too much to have? Whatever amount replaces our trust and dependence.

Jesus always deals with the heart because the heart is where trust comes from. Faith doesn't come from the mind; it comes from the heart. And bold faith stands on the shoulders of quiet trust.

> The heart that believes in him receives the gift of the righteousness of God—and then the mouth confesses, resulting in salvation.
> ROMANS 10:10 TPT

✳✳✳

What are you trusting God for in this season? How has the journey of trust been for you? Where do you find yourself turning to receive comfort in times of trouble? Take this time to tear down any strongholds of trust in your life.

A UNITED PEOPLE

I urge you, my brothers and sisters, for the sake of the name of our Lord Jesus Christ, to agree to live in unity with one another and put to rest any division that attempts to tear you apart. Be restored as one united body living in perfect harmony. Form a consistent choreography among yourselves, having a common perspective with shared values.
I CORINTHIANS 1:10 TPT

A united people can bear any pressure.

We can learn much from the early church about dealing with conflict. After being imprisoned for preaching the gospel, they left prison, "rejoicing, thrilled that God had considered them worthy to suffer disgrace for the name of Jesus. And nothing stopped them! They kept preaching every day in the temple court and went from house to house, preaching the gospel of Jesus, God's Anointed One!" (Acts 5:41-42) In the midst of persecution, they met daily in the temple and in the homes of fellow believers, drawing strength from community.

We were made to be a part of the Body of Christ. We must live accountable to other people. Without that, we are like a dislocated limb—we may be operating in our spiritual gifting, but we will be incapable of enacting lasting good for the kingdom. We can declare that we have the fruit of the Spirit, but it's only in community that we find out if that's actually true.

The disciples valued the believing community, but the church was growing quickly and some of the Greek widows were being neglected (see Acts 6:1). Until then, the conflict for the early church had all come from the outside—the Jewish council, political leaders, the synagogue—bonding the new Christian community together. For the first time, the disciples faced a challenge that had the potential to wipe out all they had accomplished together: conflict from within.

The disciples quickly addressed the situation and appointed people to meet the need, but they refused to be distracted from the call of God on their lives. A few verses later, we see the fruit of their conflict resolution: "God's word reigned supreme and kept spreading. The number of Jesus' followers in Jerusalem quickly grew and increased by the day" (Acts 6:7).

Difficulty binds people together. Where there is unity in the face of opposition, the bonds are strengthened. We've seen this evident in the wake of our own national tragedies. God didn't cause those horrific events, and He didn't cause the persecution of the early church, but He knows how to use conflict to bring unity. A united people can bear any pressure.

I therefore, a prisoner for the Lord, urge you to walk in a manner worthy of the calling to which you have been called, with all humility and gentleness, with patience, bearing with one another in love, eager to maintain the unity of the Spirit in the bond of peace.
EPHESIANS 4:1-3 ESV

***

Who holds you accountable for your actions? Who do you trust more than you trust yourself? How could you strengthen the bonds of your community in the midst of this season?

REJOICE ALWAYS

Consider it pure joy, my brothers and sisters, whenever you face trials of many kinds, because you know that the testing of your faith produces perseverance. Let perseverance finish its work so that you may be mature and complete, not lacking anything.
JAMES 1:2-4 NIV

I am someone to whom God can entrust Himself.

The muscle of integrity and character are developed as we make daily decisions in the face of challenges. When you lift weights, using a light weight may add tone, but it will not build muscle. It's only when you lift an amount that pushes the boundary of your capacity—even if you can only lift it a few times—that the most is accomplished. It's the hardest lift that builds the most strength.

Every time we face a difficult situation, there is an invitation to build our character. God never challenges us in order to shame, mock, intimidate, or humiliate us. But He does give us opportunities to become more like Christ and enter into a place of greater strength.

In I Thessalonians 5, Paul instructs us to "Rejoice always, pray continually, give thanks in all circumstances; for this is God's will for you in Christ Jesus" (verses 16-18). The most prevalent cry of our hearts is to know God's will for our lives. Often that prayer is reduced to wanting to know what God wants us to do for our career or who He wants us to marry.

Those are legitimate prayers, but God isn't as concerned about those details as He is about the posture of our hearts. That verse tells us explicitly what God's will for us is: "Rejoice always, pray continually, give thanks in all circumstances."

We could spend the rest of our lives learning how to live out those three verses. Following their instruction would be a fulltime job. To live according to God's will in this way means responding to every level of difficulty, opportunity, and challenge that comes our way with a disciplined response of joy.

Our choices, and how we respond to life's circumstances, help to develop character within us. It's our character that God wants to strengthen so we are able to carry the weightiness of what He is doing in the earth. He's looking for people to whom He can entrust Himself.

The fruit produced by the Holy Spirit within you is divine love in all its varied expressions: joy that overflows, peace that subdues, patience that endures, kindness in action, a life full of virtue, faith that prevails, gentleness of heart, and

strength of spirit. Never set the law above these qualities, for they are meant to be limitless.
GALATIANS 5:22-23 TPT

***

Have you ever responded to a situation with anything other than joy? Consider how your response, and not just the circumstance itself, affected your strength. How could you further develop the discipline of joy in your life?

IN THE SHELTER OF THE ALMIGHTY

Yahweh, you're the bedrock beneath my feet, my faith-fortress, my wonderful deliverer, my God, my rock of rescue where none can reach me. You're the shield around me, the mighty power that saves me, and my high place.
PSALM 18:2 TPT

I find shelter from the storm in the shadow of His presence.

Psalm 91 is a powerful celebration of God's protection. It begins this way: "When you abide under the shadow of Shaddai" (verse 1). This isn't merely a point of theology. When the psalmist talks about dwelling in the secret place, he is referring to a lifestyle. It is the continuous decision to maintain an awareness of the abiding Presence of the Holy Spirit. The Passion Translation describes it as living "in life-union" with God (see John 15:7). That is how we "abide under the shadow of Shaddai."

Many people stop short of a divine encounter because they are satisfied with good theology. But the Word is an invitation to meet the Person. The endeavor of our hearts is meant to be the discovery of the manifest presence of God, as surrendered sons and daughters, as yielded vessels. We must adjust our thinking, our expectations, and our prayers according to the way God thinks. He's not intimidated by anything.

When we are battling fear or dealing with a challenging circumstance, it can feel like we are stuck in the dark, far from the light. We can interpret our circumstances through our natural perspective, mistaking the darkness for isolation and confusion. But, as Corrie Ten Boom once said, "When you are covered by His wings, it can get pretty dark." Sometimes it's dark because He's so close. Sometimes it's His nearness that causes other things to lose their focus.

Scripture says that you are in the shadow of the Almighty. So, the people who turn their affection toward the ongoing, manifestation of the abiding Presence of the Spirit, dwell in a habitation of safety. Even when it's dark, we can rest in the fact that it's only a testimony of His nearness. In the shadow of His presence, we find safe shelter from the storm.

Let me dwell in Your tent forever; Let me take refuge in the shelter of Your wings.
PSALM 61:4 NASB

***

When you've been in a dark season, how have you experienced God's nearness? How

have you felt His protective presence over you? Remind yourself of the ways God has met you—through encounters with Him or even through the love of others—when you were struggling.

SUPERNATURAL HOPE

"For I know the plans and thoughts that I have for you," says the LORD, "plans for peace and well-being and not for disaster, to give you a future and a hope."
JEREMIAH 29:11 AMP

I have every reason to hope because the Hope of the Nations lives within me.

None of us know the ways of God enough to dissect how He is going to bring us into the breakthrough we long for. We all probably have testimonies of the Lord answering seemingly insignificant prayers while we are still contending for the big breakthrough.

Yet, every single answer to prayer—no matter how small—every fulfilled dream or desire, all the satisfaction we receive in life, they all reveal the truth of God. The earth is crying out to know the Father for who He truly is. We owe people a life that exudes extreme hope.

The biblical word *hope* is very different than our current cultural usage. We often use hope as synonymous with wish: *I hope there's a parking spot. I hope that person calls me. I hope that job opportunity opens up.* Biblical hope, however, is something much stronger.

Hope, in Scripture, can be translated as the joyful anticipation of good. In other words, when we have hope, we are sitting on the edge of our seats, beside ourselves with joy, because we know what's coming our way. This hope actually becomes an atmosphere in which faith grows, an atmosphere that attracts the promises of God.

We've all experienced situations where hope seems far away. We might know enough to say the right things or give the spiritual answer or pray the correct prayers, but in our heart of hearts we come face to face with the fact that hopelessness has swallowed up a part of our life.

In Romans, Paul writes that Abraham operated in "hope against hope" (4:18). He experienced his natural hope—which limits itself to human reason—being swallowed up by divine hope, which knows no limitations. Instead of just maintaining a positive attitude about life, we are meant to move into supernatural hope. This allows us to prophetically see the purposes and plans of God in our lives. Our lives are instruments of God's will. We have every reason to hope because the Hope of the Nations lives within us.

> Living within you is the Christ who floods you with the expectation of glory! This mystery of Christ, embedded within us, becomes a heavenly treasure chest of hope filled with the riches of glory for his people, and God wants everyone to know it!

COLOSSIANS 1:27 TPT

***

What have you been hoping for? In what ways could you express the joy of obtaining that desire before it is actually fulfilled? Ask God to show you His hope for your life!

NO OTHER OPTION

I am not ashamed of the gospel of Christ, for it is the power of God to salvation for everyone who believes, for the Jew first and also for the Greek.
ROMANS 1:16 NKJV

I will not bow to inferior realities because I know what God has said and done.

In Acts, Peter and John were arrested for preaching about Jesus. Dragged before court the next day, they were questioned about the power behind their bold, public teaching. Peter, filled with the Holy Spirit, shared with them about the truth of Jesus, and the religious leaders were stunned: "Now when they saw the boldness of Peter and John, and perceived that they were uneducated and untrained men, they marveled. And they realized that they had been with Jesus" (Acts 4:13).

There's something about walking with the Person of Jesus that more than compensates for every deficiency and weakness. In fact, our surrendered inability boasts of His ability. We are invited into that relationship any time we face a difficult season. In those moments, we must return to the roots of our faith: the power of the gospel of Jesus Christ.

Peter and John were commanded not to speak about Jesus, but they responded, "We cannot but speak the things which we have seen and heard" (Acts 4:20). Speaking of the things of God was not an option for Peter or John. They couldn't turn it on and off; they had glimpsed the Father. The greatest reality in the universe is the presence of the resurrected Christ. Despite being imprisoned and on trial, Peter and John refused to fill their minds with the inferior reality of their circumstance. There was no other option for them than to speak about the gospel.

Moments of trial are invitations to recommit to living without options. We were intentionally designed by the Lord for our current hour. We have been prepared—whether we feel it or not—throughout our lifetime for victory in this moment. Even if our past seems messy, every moment is now a tool in God's hands to fashion us into an instrument for righteousness on the earth. It must be said by the people of God that "we cannot help but speak" of the things we've seen and heard. We will not bow to inferior realities because we know what God has said and done.

No wonder we don't give up. For even though our outer person gradually wears out, our inner being is renewed every single day.

2 CORINTHIANS 4:16 TPT

***

What weakness do you want to surrender today so that you might see God's strength revealed? What about Him can you not help but speak about to others? Ask Him to show you how He has prepared you for the hour you are in.

DIVINE PURPOSE

Make me to know your ways, O LORD; teach me your paths. Lead me in your truth and teach me, for you are the God of my salvation; for you I wait all the day long.
PSALM 25:4-5 ESV

God's voice releases life into every situation.

Solomon is most notable for his God-given wisdom. In Proverbs, he talks about his own personal history and the priorities with which his parents raised him: "When I was a son with my father, tender, the only one in the sight of my mother, he taught me and said to me ... 'Get wisdom; get insight'" (4:1-5).

Solomon is the only person recorded in the Bible to whom God offered the choice of anything he wanted. He was the only one given that opportunity possibly because he was the only one prepared to make the right choice. David had groomed him for significance by training him in what was valuable.

So, the Lord appeared to him, and Solomon chose wisdom. If you study the original language, what Solomon actually chose was "a hearing ear." Solomon knew that God was the source of all wisdom; he just wanted to make sure he could perceive clearly what the Lord was saying.

Because his priorities were right, he received a level of wisdom that surpassed anything the world had seen before.

What's bizarre is that Solomon woke up and realized the encounter with the Lord was a dream. This means that God trusted Solomon to make a decision of that magnitude in his sleep. When we live with this kind of divine destiny, we can be completely absorbed in the reason we are alive.

In Song of Songs, Solomon wrote, "I slept, but my heart was awake" (5:2). This revelation probably came from his own history. He realized that we could sleep with such divine purpose that truth becomes a part of who we are.

Our pursuit of God's presence is not a fact that we recall or a verse that we quote, it's our reason for being. It's why we get up in the morning. It's what we go to sleep meditating on at night. No matter what challenges are surrounding us, we will lean into God with a hearing ear. We know that it's His voice that releases life into every situation.

The voice of the Lord echoes through the skies and seas. The Glory-God reigns as he thunders in the clouds. So powerful is his voice, so brilliant and bright—how majestic as he thunders over the great waters!

PSALM 29:3-4 TPT

***

What are some of the priorities with which you were raised? If you are a parent, what are some of the values you have instilled in your children? Turn your affection to God tonight before you go to bed; pray, like Solomon, for God to give you an ear that would hear Him clearly.

HIDDEN IN HIM

Here's the one thing I crave from Yahweh, the one thing I seek above all else: I want to live with him every moment in his house, beholding the marvelous beauty of Yahweh, filled with awe, delighting in his glory and grace. I want to contemplate in his temple. In the day of trouble, he will treasure me in his shelter, under the cover of his tent. He will lift me high upon a rock, out of reach from all my enemies who surround me.
PSALM 27:4-5 TPT

I cannot go into war where I have not gone first in intimacy.

The measure of spiritual authority that we use in warfare is equal to the depth of our intimacy with God in worship. There is an absolute connection throughout Scripture found in the relationship between our worship—that aggressive, demonstrated ministry to God—and the issue of having practical authority over the powers of hell and the demonic realm. Psalm 149 says, "God's high and holy praises fill their mouths, for their shouted praises are their weapons of war" (verse 6). Throughout Scripture we find that causal relationship between our praises to the Lord and the powers of hell being destroyed.

When we come into the presence of the Lord without worship, attending church as a consumer and a critic, we miss out greatly on this divine exchange. We have been given the incredible privilege of entering into a place of engagement with God. It is the privilege of our lives that we get to minister personally to Him. And the result is that as we develop our intimacy with Him, we receive a practical authority over the powers of hell.

We all have places in our lives where we haven't seen the supernatural invade in the ways we were crying out for. We know that it is God's heart to bring restoration and redemption, but we perhaps didn't see the fulfillment of His promise with a sick parent, a broken relationship, or a financial setback. We represent the King.

The key is to get before God and earnestly pray *before* you have a crisis to pray for. Anyone can pray in crisis but show me someone who will earnestly hunger for the breakthrough of God's intervention before the crisis is upon them, and I will show you someone who will solve the crisis when it comes. When we are anchored in His presence, we are prepared for any battle. But we cannot go into war where we have not gone first in intimacy.

Come close to God and He will come close to you.

JAMES 4:8 NASB

***

Where do you long to see breakthrough in your life, the lives of your family, and even in the world? How could you get to know God's heart more intimately in that area?

SOWING SEED FOR THE FUTURE

God is more than ready to overwhelm you with every form of grace, so that you will have more than enough of everything—every moment and in every way. He will make you overflow with abundance in every good thing you do.
2 CORINTHIANS 9:8 TPT

I can sow into my future because I know the God of abundance.

The Bible is filled with stories of people responding to plagues, persecution, and famine. In Genesis it says, "Now another famine struck the land, like the one in Abraham's time" (26:1). Isaac was faced with great famine and the fear for his life and that of his family that news of famine would have carried. Yet, he responded in an unusual way: "Isaac planted crops in that land, and in the same year reaped a hundredfold harvest, for Yahweh greatly blessed him!" (26:12)

Many years ago, a missionary friend in Africa sent out a newsletter. In it, he wrote that for the first time he understood what it meant when the Bible said, "Those who sow their tears as seeds will reap a harvest with joyful shouts of glee" (Psalm 126:5). He described how he saw mothers with children strapped to their backs, take the seed they were hungry to eat and make the choice to plant it in the ground, weeping as they made that decision. They knew that they could eat that seed and satisfy their family's hunger for now. But, if they planted it, it could provide a whole season of meals.

In the face of potential devastating loss, Isaac intentionally sowed into his future. He made a decision that probably would have seemed foolish to others. It's natural to want to hoard resources during a time of crisis, but instead he planted in faith.

We have every reason to hope, no matter what the circumstance. Our reason is Jesus. He has conquered every enemy, causing everything to work for good to those who love God and are called according to his purpose (see Romans 8:28). When we are surrounded by fear and doubt, we have the opportunity to respond with hope and expectation.

Seasons of famine are not times to be foolish or careless; they are opportunities to position ourselves for breakthrough. We can face the fear of lack and, instead, offer God something to breathe on. We can sow into our future because we know the God of abundance.

The land, into which you are entering to possess it, is not like the land of Egypt from which you came, where you used to sow your seed and

water it by your foot like a vegetable garden. But the land into which you are about to cross to possess it, a land of hills and valleys, drinks water from the rain of heaven, a land for which the LORD your God cares; the eyes of the LORD your God are continually on it, from the beginning even to the end of the year.
DEUTERONOMY 11:10-12 NASB

***

How does it feel to hear about Isaac and the women from Africa sowing seeds in the midst of a famine? What could sowing into your future look like for you in this moment? How could you take a stand of hope and faith, trusting in the God of abundance?

BEAUTY FOR ASHES

I am sent to announce a new season of Yahweh's grace and a time of God's recompense on his enemies, to comfort all who are in sorrow, to strengthen those crushed by despair who mourn in Zion—to give them a beautiful bouquet in the place of ashes, the oil of bliss instead of tears, and the mantle of joyous praise instead of the spirit of heaviness.
ISAIAH 61:2-3 TPT

No matter what, God will be glorified and I will be strengthened.

The Christian faith is founded on the resurrection of Jesus. Paul said that if our faith in Christ is only in this life, "we deserve to be pitied more than all others!" (1 Corinthians 15:19) That Jesus triumphed over death is the rock-solid foundation of our faith. But not only was He raised from the dead, He set the precedent for resurrection with His lifestyle. He ruined every funeral He attended including His own.

We must refuse to hold God hostage to what we want in any given situation. He is God; we are His sons and daughters. We are His servants. But He is the One who instructed us to pursue the reality of heaven. He told us to "constantly seek God's kingdom" (Matthew 6:33). What does the kingdom look like? It's not the pursuit of going to heaven. It's the pursuit of God's solutions for death, loss, and destruction here on earth.

The kingdom of God manifested on earth is the immediate expression of God's dominion in any given situation. Where there's death, He brings resurrection. Where there's brokenness in relationships, He brings healing. Where there's disease, He brings restoration of the body. Our responsibility is to seek first and foremost God's solution, His supernatural intervention, in every circumstance. This is the privilege of saying yes to Jesus.

We have a promise in Scripture that "every detail of our lives is continually woven together for good, for we are his lovers who have been called to fulfill his designed purpose" (Romans 8:28). That verse would be completely unnecessary if circumstances lined up just as we wanted every time we prayed. The only reason that promise was given to us is because sometimes we're going to swing and miss. Sometimes we're going to pursue resurrection in an area of our life, and the breakthrough won't come. But we have God's promise that when things don't happen as we prayed they would, God will still be glorified and we will be strengthened. No matter what.

"I will bring my exiled people of Israel back from distant lands, and they will rebuild their ruined cities and live in them again. They will plant vineyards and gardens; they will eat their crops and drink their wine."
AMOS 9:14 NLT

***

How does knowing this promise—that you will be strengthened and God will be glorified—reframe your thinking about any current disappointments. Where are you waiting to see God's resurrection power? Place those things in His hands, knowing that if it's not good yet, it's not the end of your story.

THE PEACE OF GOD

Brothers and sisters, whatever is true, whatever is honorable, whatever is right, whatever is pure, whatever is lovely, whatever is commendable, if there is any excellence and if anything worthy of praise, think about these things. As for the things you have learned and received and heard and seen in me, practice these things, and the God of peace will be with you.
PHILIPPIANS 4:8-9 NASB

Peace is my possession; it is my birthright in Christ.

    The enemy tries to sow anxiety into several aspects of a believer's life. First, he works to keep us exposed to anxiety and stress because it undermines our creativity. When we are living in anxiety and stress, our focus is limited to survival; there is no room for creative expression. The Lord longs to express who He is—His own nature, His beauty and creativity—through a yielded believer. To do this, we have to be free of anxiety and stress.
    Secondly, the enemy tries to derail our first love relationship with the Lord. We can't be anxious and keep the kind of fervent relationship with the Lord for which all of us long. Anxiety exalts an inferior truth over the Word of the

Lord and all that He has promised. It is true that love annihilates fear, but it's also true that if we embrace fear, we have allowed something into our lives that will infect love. Our first love relationship with Jesus is the most important aspect of our lives (see Revelation 2).

Finally, the enemy wants to undermine our sense of identity. Fear and anxiety cause us to lose track of the tools and the authority God has given to us. It is possible to live free from anxiety and stress. Jesus showed us this by going to the cross giving thanks. In this, He illustrated something so profound. He didn't just keep a stiff upper lip. He operated in His identity as an overcomer. He went into a hellish situation and came out absolutely glorious.

If we lose our peace, we need to find out where we exchanged it for an inferior perspective. Peace in the kingdom is very profound. It's the abiding presence of the Spirit of God in our lives. He will never abandon us, but our felt awareness of Him can get laid aside. In the kingdom of heaven, we can be in the middle of any kind of crisis and maintain peace because peace is a Person. Peace is our possession; it is our birthright in Christ.

To us a child is born, to us a son is given, and the government will be on his shoulders. And he will be called Wonderful Counselor, Mighty God, Everlasting Father, Prince of Peace.
ISAIAH 9:6 NIV

✱✱✱

Have you experienced the attempts of the enemy to sow fear and anxiety into areas of your life? The peace of God is legally yours, so how can you go back and regain your peace if you lose it? How do you most clearly experience the tangible presence of peace Himself?

CALL UPON THE LORD

"If you remain in Me and My words remain in you [that is, if we are vitally united and My message lives in your heart], ask whatever you wish and it will be done for you."
JOHN 15:7 AMP

I was designed to live a life of miracles, revealing God's heart to the world.

We were designed for answered prayer. To not receive the breakthrough that we're crying out for is abnormal. The disciples knew this when they couldn't cast the demon out of the child (see Matthew 17:19). When we pray, we can't assume a lack of breakthrough is the will of God. The Bible says, "He will call upon Me, and I will answer him" (Psalm 91:15). That's the promise. So, if we haven't seen breakthrough, we need to ask God what He's doing.

Each one of us started our life in Christ with that exchange. Take away all of our spiritual gifts, all of our history with God, and we all have one common denominator: we called upon the Lord, He heard us, and He saved us. Our life in Christ began with an answer to prayer. When we cried out to God, He performed the greatest miracle we will ever see in our life—the salvation of our souls. Our lives began with the miraculous, and that foundation was never meant to decline.

God promises us, "I will be with him in trouble; I will rescue him and honor him. With a long life I will satisfy him and I will let him see My salvation" (Psalm 91:15-16). God doesn't say we won't experience difficult times. In fact, this verse specifically says that sometimes we will be in trouble. But He is with us. The table of fellowship is there in His presence, and He doesn't just promise to set us free and protect us. He will honor us as one of His own. He marks us with His blessing and rewards us with a long life.

The verse does not promise us a long life in terms of merely surviving. God promises us a long life given to satisfy. Our life in Christ was never meant to be reduced to enduring the routine of Christian discipline and fellowship. We were designed for the adventure of faith, bringing in the harvest for His glory. We were designed to live a life of miracles, revealing God's heart to the world.

"Keep on asking, and you will receive what you ask for. Keep on seeking, and you will find. Keep on knocking, and the door will be opened to you."

MATTHEW 7:7 NLT

***

What miracle are you contending for right now? Even if you're not experiencing breakthrough in that area yet, where are you seeing God move in your life? How are you hearing His voice and in what ways are you experiencing His love?

PETER'S PRAYER

The fading ministry came with a portion of glory, but now we embrace the unfading ministry of a permanent impartation of glory. So then, with this amazing hope living in us, we step out in freedom and boldness to speak the truth.
2 CORINTHIANS 3:11-12 TPT

God, give me all boldness!

In the fourth chapter of Acts, Peter prayed one of the most courageous prayers found in the Bible. The boldness with which he preached the gospel had already been recognized (verse 13). Yet, when he and John were imprisoned and threatened, Peter didn't pray for fancier words or even for God to rescue them from their situation. He prayed for even greater boldness. He asked God to turn up the heat, to give them more of the very thing that got them thrown into prison in the first place.

Sometimes, when we're faced with opposition, we can become fearful and timid. We fall into the trap of compromising our faith in order to avoid conflict. What we truly need in those seasons, though, is a greater measure of boldness. We never want to be purposefully offensive or obnoxious in our manner, but we need the kind of courage that stands up in the face of unbelief and declares who Jesus is and what He has promised to us.

There is a story about a test pilot in the UK who took a new plane up in the air. Its interior was still in an unfinished state, so the wiring and tubing was exposed. Suddenly, the pilot noticed that there was a rat on the plane that was chewing on a fuel line. The pilot, knowing he didn't have time to land safely, took the plane higher. He knew that he had oxygen, but the rat didn't. So, he took the plane up to an elevation where the rat could not survive.

When we notice a rat onboard—an obstacle or lie from the enemy, trying to invade our God-given destiny—it's not time to land the plane. We need to climb higher. In difficult seasons, we don't need a palatable gospel; we need the fullness of Jesus Christ to be on display. Every problem we face is an invitation from God to go higher, becoming even more of who we're meant to be in Him. We need the prayer of Peter: God, give us all boldness.

> The wicked flee when no one pursues, but the righteous are bold as a lion.
> PROVERBS 28:1 ESV

***

In what areas of your life, or with whom, have you experienced the fear of man?

154

What opposition are you facing today? What would "all boldness" look like for you? How could you take your plane higher, suffocating any lies from the enemy?

GOD OF ABUNDANCE

"The LORD bless you and keep you; the LORD make his face to shine upon you and be gracious to you; the LORD lift up his countenance upon you and give you peace."
NUMBERS 6:24-26 ESV

I am a part of an army of world-changers defining the nature of the world because of the hope I carry.

Our cry for you is that in every single area of life, every place where hopelessness has influenced you would die and be swallowed up with divine promise and hope. God has never been the God of just enough. He created too much food every time He fed the multitudes (see Matthew 14:20). We were never meant to have our sights set on just barely making it.

We pray that divine hope would consume natural hope in the area of personal finances. We pray that there would be a spirit of breakthrough brought into the lives of those who greatly need to experience economic release.

We pray over your family relationships, that this next season would be the season of restored hope for lost family members, those dealing with illness, or family members who are in crisis. Jesus is the One who restores broken hearts and broken minds. There is not one unredeemable situation in our family line.

We pray for the dreams of your heart, those desires that are so buried that they're almost embarrassing to talk about. We pray that this would be the season that God breathes on the impossibilities of life. The Bible says that the kingdom of God is like a mustard seed (see Matthew 13:31). A mustard seed is not very impressive. Put it on the table, and it won't do a thing. But put it into the right environment, and it will grow until it creates a place of refuge for other creatures. There is a kingdom expression in you longing to get planted. When it does, you will provide safety, shelter, and protection for others. The world is crying out for the fullness of who you are to become manifest.

We pray that this contagious hope would absolutely immerse your home, your city, and your nation. That you would become part of an army of world-changers defining the nature of the world you live in because of the hope that you carry. Amen.

I kneel humbly in awe before the Father of our Lord Jesus, the Messiah, the perfect Father of every father and child in heaven and on the earth. And I pray that he would unveil within you the unlimited riches of his glory and favor until supernatural strength floods your innermost being with his divine might and explosive power.

EPHESIANS 3:14-16 TPT

***

Write out declarations over your life, over your finances, over your relationships, and over the desires of your heart. What do you want to see come to pass? Review the promises of God throughout Scripture and take them as your own. Let contagious hope surround you!

BILL & BENI JOHNSON
are the senior leaders of Bethel Church in Redding, California, teaching and equipping people to live a supernatural lifestyle. Together, they serve a growing number of churches worldwide that are passionate for revival and seeing God's kingdom established on earth.

BACK COVER MATERIAL

"I LEAVE THE GIFT OF PEACE WITH YOU—MY PEACE. NOT THE KIND OF FRAGILE PEACE GIVEN BY THE WORLD, BUT MY PERFECT PEACE."
JOHN 14:27 TPT

www.ingramcontent.com/pod-product-compliance
Lightning Source LLC
Chambersburg PA
CBHW011944150426
43192CB00017B/2779